STUNNED BY GRIEF

JOURNAL

Also available from this author

***STUNNED** by Grief:*
Remapping Your Life When Loss Changes Everything

STUNNED BY GRIEF *JOURNAL*

Judy Brizendine

BennettKnepp
PUBLISHING

Lake Forest, CA

STUNNED by Grief Journal

Published by BennettKnepp Publishing, P.O. Box 296, Lake Forest, CA 92609-0296

Questions or requests for information should be addressed to the publisher:
info@bennettknepp.com

Cover and Page Design by DesignForBooks.com
Leather texture on cover: iStock©milosluz
Editor: Susan Malone, Malone Editorial Services
Page 209: author photo credit © Jon Kreider

Disclaimer

Information within this book does not constitute medical, psychological, or other professional advice. If expert assistance is required, the services of a competent professional should be sought. The ideas and suggestions in this book are intended to supplement, not replace, the advice of a trained professional. The purchaser of this book assumes full responsibility for the use of this information. The Publisher and Author assume no liability either directly or indirectly from advice contained within, or actions taken because of, information contained in this book.

ISBN 10: 0983168806
ISBN 13: 978-0-9831688-0-5

PRINTED IN THE UNITED STATES OF AMERICA

DEDICATION

To each person who opens this journal,
reads the words, and takes action

CONTENTS

INTRODUCTION

LOSS. GRIEF. REMAPPING.

This journal may be different from similar journals you have seen. It contains 'bits' to read (and think about), lots of room to write, and is a companion to my book, *STUNNED by Grief: Remapping Your Life When Loss Changes Everything.* This journal is for *writing.*

Journaling is a key tool in remapping, and this book will guide you along the path. Here's how the journal works:

Man is born broken. He lives by mending. The grace of God is glue.

—Eugene O'Neill

- Pages are not dated—but you can enter the date, if you wish. Start at any time of the year, on any day.
- Take a moment each day as you begin and do a "feelings" check. Write your answer. When you look back over your journal weeks or months later, being aware of your frame of mind will increase your understanding and help to gauge your progress.
  (If you need help identifying your feelings, turn to the checklist in the Appendix of your journal.)
- Each day you will find a thought pertaining to loss, grief, or remapping. If you are unsure what to write about that day, use this thought as a catalyst to get started.

- Think of *one thing* every day that you are thankful for and write it down. Gratitude is healthy—and powerful. It is also positive!
- A specially selected Bible verse or quote related to the day's thought appears on each journal page. Read the verse (or quote) and think about it. Listen for what God wants to say to you.
- I have written a short note to you each day (under Reflections) with insights from my own grief experience. Take these notes to heart, and remind yourself that someone else understands what you are going through. You are not alone. While I cannot be right there with you, I can communicate with you each day through these words.
- Blank pages have been included at the back of the journal. Add a question or thought of your own and a special Bible verse, if you wish. Write about whatever comes to mind. These pages are for you.

The most important thing you can do is to *start writing.* Write about what is tearing at your heart, what you can't stop thinking about, what keeps you awake at night, makes you angry, frightens you, confuses you, what you're grateful for . . . or *whatever* is on your mind.

Don't worry about how your writing looks, whether it is grammatically correct, how it sounds, or even whether it makes sense. Just write. And be *honest.* Don't edit what you say.

Writing about your thoughts, questions, concerns, feelings, and fears will help you process your grief and remap your life. Journaling helps you reach a place of acceptance, release, and renewal.

The goal is to work through what is on the inside, so you can bring it to the outside and release it. Write about whatever is on your mind.

I encourage you to write, as little or as much as you want, every day, if possible. Just write!

If you miss a day or two (or even more), don't beat yourself up. Pick up where you left off and start again.

Think of me as a coach or a companion, standing beside you, walking along with you, encouraging and reassuring you every step of the way.

I have already been down this road. I know the path. I want to help you, and so does God.

Just start the journey, and use this journal as a tool—a means of helping you to go from where you are to where you want to be. You may be surprised what happens.

As you write, your journal will become a treasured collection of thoughts telling the story of who you are, where you have been, what you've learned, who you are becoming, and where you are going—by the Grace of God.

Hope is grief's best music.
—Anonymous

I pray that you will find courage, peace, healing, and new joy as you go forward. Thank you for letting me walk beside you.

Judy Brizendine

Judy Brizendine

REMAPPING

Life is a succession of crises and moments when we have to rediscover who we are and what we really want.

—Jean Vanier

A word picture and an image can illustrate a griever's evolving path as he or she moves through grief toward healing (remapping). Visualize a slightly flattened diamond shape with rounded corners, but one that does not connect end-to-end. Instead, the line completing the outline of the diamond extends just beyond (and slightly outside) the original starting point near its base, an important distinction you will see in a moment. This line runs parallel to the original one for a short distance—and points upward with an arrow at its end. 'Ripples' fill the diamond's interior. This visual summarizes the remapping process. It is a symbol of hope. Plant the picture in your mind. Recall its meaning expressed below. And remember your destination.

Remapping—a Symbol of Hope

At first, because of intense, unrelenting pain, one's focus is completely self-centered and stuck on square one. After a while, even though you have started moving around the course, you *feel* as though you're going backward. As you start to heal, *slowly* your focus becomes less self-absorbed. Gradually, as you travel farther along, you realize you *are* moving forward. In time, your attention shifts from the past (and loss) to the future. You become more sensitive to people around you [the ripple effect].

Grief's uneven path—marked by ins and outs, ups and downs—does not fit a perfectly predictable pattern. So instead of a circle, a diamond-like shape represents a more accurate picture of the remapping process.

Eventually, to complete the healing process we all need to move full circle—and finally emerge on the other side of grief. However, we don't end up in the places where we started. Instead, we end up *beyond* our starting points—and on slightly different paths (the continuing parallel line, just outside the position where the diamond began). An upward-arcing arrow at the end of the line signifies a new beginning.

After confronting the pain of loss, our perspectives change forever, and our capacities to be human deepen. We now see life through different lenses.

The very least you can do in your life is to figure out what you hope for. And the most you can do is live inside that hope. Not admire it from a distance but live right in it, under its roof.

—Barbara Kingsolver

Concern and empathy develop out of our experiences of loss, and the prospect of helping others because of what we have learned and endured becomes a consideration, possibly even a passion. Ironically, helping others is personally healing. By reaching out to help other people, we are also doing something healthy for ourselves.

When I look for ways to encourage someone else, I temporarily forget about my concerns. When my actions make someone's day better or ease her worry, my attitude *sings*. We both win.

Looking for the blessings that come from pain requires effort, attention, and time. We will not even want to entertain this thought when our pain is fresh and deep. However, having endured the anguish, we long for something positive to come out of it.

There *must* be some purpose in the pain. The purpose is twofold—insight for living life more fully and a deeper relationship with God.

My Journey

TODAY:

FEELINGS CHECK
Today I feel:

ONE THING I'M GRATEFUL FOR TODAY:

REFLECTIONS

Tragedy generally strikes when we are just living life, doing what we always do—and we're taken by surprise, caught off-guard. God offers genuine reasons for hope in the middle of your turmoil and solid ground where you can confidently plant your feet. There is a path through grief. Let's walk down this path together. I will do my best to show you the way.

TODAY'S THOUGHT

Life changes when (and how) we least expect.

BIBLE VERSE

PROVERBS 24:22 (*MSG*)

Without warning your life can turn upside-down, and who knows how or when it might happen?

TODAY'S THOUGHT

Grief is not what we expect and its reality is nothing we can imagine.

TODAY:

FEELINGS CHECK
Today I feel:

ONE THING I'M GRATEFUL FOR TODAY:

BIBLE VERSE

LAMENTATIONS 3:20–22 (*NLT*)

I will never forget this awful time, as I grieve over my loss. Yet I still dare to hope when I remember this: The unfailing love of the Lord never ends! . . .

REFLECTIONS

When my husband died, I had no idea what grief was, how it was supposed to feel, what to do with it, or what was normal. Grief is not what I expected. But I learned about it because I wanted to be okay again. Gratefully, I pass on to you what I learned *under fire*. In time, you will be okay, too. Your pain seems unbearable right now, but keep remembering the hope you have in God. His love is *real*, and it will never go away. Never.

TODAY:

FEELINGS CHECK
Today I feel:

ONE THING
I'M GRATEFUL
FOR TODAY:

TODAY'S THOUGHT

Instantly, my entire world and the way I related to my world changed. The change was far-reaching.

BIBLE VERSE

Isaiah 40:11 (*NLT*)

He will feed his flock like a shepherd. He will carry the lambs in his arms, holding them close to his heart . . .

REFLECTIONS

Grief invaded my life, and when my world turned completely upside down, verses like this one were a lifeline—and a promise of peace and security. Realizing God sees us as precious lambs that He carries close to His heart comforted me, especially during the upheaval and uncertainty of grief. He wants to comfort you, too.

TODAY'S THOUGHT

I can tell you with absolute confidence there *is* hope, even during the darkest, seemingly hopeless times of grief. Trust me. Trust Him!

TODAY: ________

FEELINGS CHECK
Today I feel:

ONE THING I'M GRATEFUL FOR TODAY:

BIBLE VERSE

II CORINTHIANS 4:8–9 (*MSG*)

We've been surrounded and battered by troubles, but we're not demoralized; we're not sure what to do, but we know that God knows what to do; we've been spiritually terrorized, but God hasn't left our side; we've been thrown down, but we haven't broken.

REFLECTIONS

As long as you are alive, there is hope. Hope permeates life and inspires each of us. It must be part of our DNA . . . but even so, our greatest hope is in *God.* Sometimes situations smother or confuse our hope. However, even when we cannot see it, hope is still there *fighting* to be heard. Listen for its sound.

TODAY: ________

FEELINGS CHECK
Today I feel:

ONE THING I'M GRATEFUL FOR TODAY:

TODAY'S THOUGHT

Grief—in the beginning is all consuming; a multitude of tangled emotions; and overwhelming, indescribable pain.

BIBLE VERSE

PSALM 22:24 (*MSG*)

He has never let you down, never looked the other way when you were being kicked around. He has never wandered off to do his own thing; he has been right there, listening.

REFLECTIONS

Your pain is undeniable. You may feel alone, want to be alone, or fear being alone. However, you can be confident that God has not abandoned you, even though you may *feel* as though He has. Do not trust your feelings where God is concerned. Feelings are an unreliable, misguided gauge of the truth, and your feelings will deceive you.

TODAY'S THOUGHT

Grief, as it evolves, is a journey through unknown territory. At times, you feel as though your life is on *autopilot*—and disconnected.

TODAY: ________

FEELINGS CHECK
Today I feel:

ONE THING I'M GRATEFUL FOR TODAY:

BIBLE VERSE

PSALM 34:18 (*NLT*)

The Lord is close to the brokenhearted; he rescues those who are crushed in spirit.

REFLECTIONS

You may feel disconnected from life and people, but God is not detached from you. He's aware of everything, He sees your turmoil, and He cares. *Autopilot* conjures up an image of living without energy, interest, or passion. I was lost as though in a fog—distracted, confused, and uncertain. I *needed* people, but sometimes I could not stand to be near anyone. Puzzling and contradictory? Yes. But it is an accurate picture, *at times*, during grief.

TODAY: ______

FEELINGS CHECK
Today I feel:

ONE THING I'M GRATEFUL FOR TODAY:

TODAY'S THOUGHT

The need to talk, the need to be heard, and the need to know someone *really* cares are effects of grief.

BIBLE VERSE

PROVERBS 18:20 (*NLT*)

Words satisfy the soul as food satisfies the stomach; the right words on a person's lips bring satisfaction.

REFLECTIONS

You may think no one understands you—or the effects of your grief. Additionally, grief can be lonely, though at times you need to be alone. Talking about your loss will not only help you cope with the pain, but will connect you to others. Someone may not always be available when you need to talk, but you can talk to God anytime—and He is always there, waiting and willing to listen.

TODAY'S THOUGHT

You will make sense of the chaos of grief in your unique way, by your own timetable, along with those you choose to walk the path beside you.

TODAY: ______

FEELINGS CHECK
Today I feel:

ONE THING I'M GRATEFUL FOR TODAY:

BIBLE VERSE

ECCLESIASTES 3:1, 4–6 (*MSG*)

There's an opportune time to do things, a right time for everything on the earth: . . .
A right time to cry and another to laugh . . .
A right time to embrace and another to part . . .
A right time to hold on and another to let go . . .

REFLECTIONS

Grieving is normal, and you should be free to grieve in your own way and in your own time. Do not let others make you feel guilty because they think you are not moving quickly enough; you're crying too much or too little; or you're not doing this or that. Grieving is natural, healthy, and *individual.* There is no right or wrong way—it's *your grief, your way.*

TODAY: ______

FEELINGS CHECK
Today I feel:

ONE THING I'M GRATEFUL FOR TODAY:

TODAY'S THOUGHT

Write about the details of your loss. Describe what happened and how you feel.

BIBLE VERSE

I Peter 5:7 (*NLT*)

Give all your worries and cares to God, for he cares about what happens to you.

REFLECTIONS

Talking and writing about your loss are immeasurably helpful. When you talk and write about it, you're *facing* your grief and gradually working through it—so you will finally be able to release your loved one and your loss. Step by step, you're adding building blocks to your healing, and steadily you're moving forward. Remember, you are not competing in a race, and this is not a sprint to the finish line.

TODAY'S THOUGHT

Grief will test everything you have within yourself—and more.

TODAY: ________

FEELINGS CHECK
Today I feel:

ONE THING I'M GRATEFUL FOR TODAY:

BIBLE VERSE

JAMES 1:3–4 (*NLT*)

For when your faith is tested, your endurance has a chance to grow. So let it grow, for when your endurance is fully developed, you will be strong in character and ready for anything.

REFLECTIONS

Grief is hard, but it *is* doable, and you will grow stronger because of your journey. Difficult times build strength and endurance, and the fight to go on builds character. I do not doubt that you are stronger than you think. Perhaps nothing has tested you the way grief is testing you now. Repeatedly, I have seen grieving people do things they did not think they could possibly do, and so can you. Trust me.

TODAY:

FEELINGS CHECK
Today I feel:

ONE THING I'M GRATEFUL FOR TODAY:

TODAY'S THOUGHT

Until my husband died, I was just like anyone else who had not experienced grief. I had no concept of the far-reaching effects of a major loss.

BIBLE VERSE

II CORINTHIANS 1:4 (*NLT*)

He comforts us in all our troubles so that we can comfort others. When others are troubled, we will be able to give them the same comfort God has given us.

REFLECTIONS

Loss affects *every* area of one's life. Grief affects us physically, mentally, emotionally, relationally, and spiritually. It affects our present and our future. We need the comfort of God and each other, and *no one* understands as does someone who has been there. Talk to someone who has already faced grief, and after you receive help, turn around and do the same for someone else.

TODAY'S THOUGHT

We must grieve so we can be
happy again—because
grief does not just go away.

TODAY: ________

FEELINGS CHECK
Today I feel:

ONE THING I'M GRATEFUL FOR TODAY:

BIBLE VERSE

Psalm 126:4–6 (*MSG*)

And now, God, do it again—bring rains to our drought-stricken lives
So those who planted their crops in despair will shout hurrahs at the harvest,
So those who went off with heavy hearts will come home laughing, with armloads of blessing.

REFLECTIONS

Grieving your loss allows you to free yourself from the pain, so you can open your heart and experience happiness again. Until you have worked through the pain, you cannot successfully get on with your life. You cannot embrace the joy of new experiences and relationships until the pain heals.

TODAY:

FEELINGS CHECK
Today I feel:

ONE THING I'M GRATEFUL FOR TODAY:

TODAY'S THOUGHT

Each person's grief is distinctive and personal, but grieving is common to everyone. Still, individual reactions vary drastically.

BIBLE VERSE

NUMBERS 6:24–26 (*NLT*)

'May the Lord bless you and protect you. May the Lord smile on you and be gracious to you. May the Lord show you his favor and give you his peace.'

REFLECTIONS

Everyone reacts differently to grief. Even Jesus cried. But some people are unable to cry; others have difficulty talking; some refuse to admit they are grieving; and others are overly emotional. Some responses may contradict your usual temperament or behavior. Each person grieves in his own way.

TODAY'S THOUGHT

Grievers do not need to be fixed, but they need to be heard. And they need to be heard more than once.

TODAY: ______

FEELINGS CHECK
Today I feel:

ONE THING I'M GRATEFUL FOR TODAY:

BIBLE VERSE

CORINTHIANS 13:4–5, 7 (*NLT*)

Love is patient and kind . . . Love does not demand its own way. Love is not irritable, and it keeps no record of when it has been wronged . . .

Love never gives up, never loses faith, is always hopeful, and endures through every circumstance.

REFLECTIONS

Grievers need *someone* to listen, and once is *not* enough. Talking about your loss one time does not heal grief—your pain is far too deep for instant healing. Grieving requires action by you, gradual and repeated action over time.

TODAY:

FEELINGS CHECK
Today I feel:

ONE THING I'M GRATEFUL FOR TODAY:

TODAY'S THOUGHT

Tragic loss will test your strength, character, and beliefs.

BIBLE VERSE

PROVERBS 4:23 (*NLT*)

Above all else, guard your heart, for it affects everything you do.

REFLECTIONS

Something good can emerge from your grief, if you choose that path. Watch over your heart, examine your thoughts, and do not allow negative thinking to trap you. Painful, demanding circumstances test your ability to stay positive and keep going. But put one foot in front of the other, *ignoring your speed*, and continue. Focus on God instead of yourself and your condition, and He *will* help you. His power will enable you to do what you cannot do alone.

TODAY'S THOUGHT

For your own mental health and ability to cope, you may need to withdraw from certain activities and relationships for a while. Do you need to step away from anyone or anything?

TODAY: ______

FEELINGS CHECK
Today I feel:

ONE THING I'M GRATEFUL FOR TODAY:

BIBLE VERSE

PROVERBS 3:18 (*NLT*)

Wisdom is a tree of life to those who embrace her; happy are those who hold her tightly.

REFLECTIONS

During the challenging time of grief, if people or activities drag you down, distance yourself from them—at least for a while. Especially now, surround yourself with those who inspire and support you—people who help you and do not cause additional pain or hamper your progress. Take special care of yourself because you are more vulnerable than usual.

TODAY: ________

FEELINGS CHECK
Today I feel:

ONE THING I'M GRATEFUL FOR TODAY:

TODAY'S THOUGHT

Grief affects a person physically, mentally, emotionally, relationally, and spiritually. Grief affects every area of one's life.

BIBLE VERSE

PSALM 25:15 (*MSG*)

If I keep my eyes on God, I won't trip over my own feet.

REFLECTIONS

Keep reminding yourself that grief will not last forever . . . it will *not* last forever. When distress overwhelms all areas of your life, remaining optimistic and staying objective is a challenge. Weariness will likely chase after you, but you *can* make it through. I made it, despite my uncertainty, and others have come through, too. So can you. Believe it!

TODAY'S THOUGHT

Unresolved grief is harmful to your future health and happiness. Discuss any unresolved losses.

TODAY: ______

FEELINGS CHECK
Today I feel:

ONE THING I'M GRATEFUL FOR TODAY:

BIBLE VERSE

Proverbs 18:14 (*NLT*)

The human spirit can endure a sick body, but who can bear it if the spirit is crushed?

REFLECTIONS

Unresolved loss is cumulative, and it is harmful. To improve your overall well-being and promote healthy relationships, the reasons for effectively dealing with grief are convincing. I have seen lives miserably troubled because people failed to deal with grief. Do not allow one tragedy or loss to create another. Do what you must do to get well.

TODAY:

FEELINGS CHECK
Today I feel:

ONE THING I'M GRATEFUL FOR TODAY:

TODAY'S THOUGHT

Grief is
not your enemy.

BIBLE VERSE

Psalm 56:8 (*NLT*)

You keep track of all my sorrows. You have collected all my tears in your bottle. You have recorded each one in your book.

REFLECTIONS

God knows all you have been through, and He never fails to remember. Grief teaches you unforgettable lessons because your perspective will forever change. You will see life differently, and the change *can* be positive. Grief is not your enemy—in fact, while you would never have chosen your situation, look for what you can learn from it. Instead of resisting where you are, try to find *something* positive to bring out of it. I *know* something positive is there.

TODAY'S THOUGHT

The pain of grief never disappears completely, but if you refuse to give up, and allow healing to take place, God will bring something valuable out of your sorrow.

TODAY: ______

FEELINGS CHECK
Today I feel:

ONE THING I'M GRATEFUL FOR TODAY:

BIBLE VERSE

PSALM 130:5 (*NLT*)

I am counting on the Lord; yes, I am counting on him. I have put my hope in his word.

REFLECTIONS

God will bring something good from your pain, *if* you will let Him. Others have discovered this truth, and so can you. Subtle reminders of your loss will be with you always, but the intensity of your grief will gradually weaken, and cherished memories will replace the sharp pain. *Decide* not to give up!

TODAY:

FEELINGS CHECK
Today I feel:

ONE THING I'M GRATEFUL FOR TODAY:

TODAY'S THOUGHT

People sometimes avoid grief and grievers because they do not know what to do or say. What have you experienced?

BIBLE VERSE

PSALM 31:11–12 (*NLT*)

. . . even my friends are afraid to come near me. When they see me on the street, they turn the other way. I have been ignored as if I were dead, as if I were a broken pot.

REFLECTIONS

Sometimes people want to help grievers, but because they do not understand, they are afraid of doing (or saying) the wrong thing. They are uneasy and embarrassed because they don't know what they *can* do. Help your loved ones by telling them what you need. Let them know *how* they can help. By doing this, you will find the support you need, and they will finally be equipped to help. Everyone wins.

TODAY'S THOUGHT

Do not be afraid to talk about your loved one and your loss, and do not be afraid to cry.

TODAY: ______

FEELINGS CHECK
Today I feel:

ONE THING I'M GRATEFUL FOR TODAY:

BIBLE VERSE

PSALM 142:1–3 (*NLT*)

I cry out to the Lord . . . I pour out my complaints before him and tell him all my troubles. For I am overwhelmed, and you alone know the way I should turn . . .

REFLECTIONS

Talking and crying are *essential actions* on the way to healing from grief. Do not be afraid to talk or cry. Of course, be discerning about where and with whom you share your grief, but talking and crying are ways to confront and work through your pain. Freeing pent-up thoughts, concerns, and emotions provides relief. If you are uncomfortable, remind yourself that grieving is a *natural process*. Eventually, everyone will experience grief.

TODAY: ________

FEELINGS CHECK
Today I feel:

ONE THING I'M GRATEFUL FOR TODAY:

TODAY'S THOUGHT

People who have not lived through grief think you should be over it in a few short weeks, or at most, a few short months.

BIBLE VERSE

PSALM 40:2 (*NLT*)

He lifted me out of the pit of despair, out of the mud and the mire. He set my feet on solid ground and steadied me as I walked along.

REFLECTIONS

People who have not grieved cannot comprehend your grief. Do not be pressured to grieve the way others *think* you should, especially those unacquainted with its course. Give grieving *the time it takes.* Try not to become impatient with yourself, and remember, it's a process . . . *a progression* . . . a series of changes over time.

TODAY'S THOUGHT

Unexpected sources may provide a griever's most beneficial support.

BIBLE VERSE

LAMENTATIONS 3:25 (*NLT*)

The Lord is wonderfully good to those who wait for him and seek him.

TODAY: ______

FEELINGS CHECK
Today I feel:

ONE THING I'M GRATEFUL FOR TODAY:

REFLECTIONS

God is always there for you, but you may be surprised to find help from someone you hardly know. No substitute exists for someone else who has faced profound loss. Grievers *understand* other grievers. *Nothing* can imitate experience where grief is concerned.

TODAY: ______

FEELINGS CHECK
Today I feel:

ONE THING I'M GRATEFUL FOR TODAY:

TODAY'S THOUGHT

Grief sometimes alters relationships, even long-term or family connections.

BIBLE VERSE

PSALM 5:11 (*MSG*)

But you'll welcome us with open arms when we run for cover to you.

REFLECTIONS

Relationships may suddenly change [without explanation] because a loved one dies or a major loss occurs, and the outcome may disappoint you. Others are busy with their lives and problems. At first, your tragedy is a top concern, but before long, its urgency fades. God will always be there for you, even when others forget. You can cry and protest to God, and He *always* listens. He will never abandon you.

TODAY'S THOUGHT

Do not try to hurry grieving. And don't let others set your timetable. Take the time you need.

TODAY: ______

FEELINGS CHECK
Today I feel:

ONE THING I'M GRATEFUL FOR TODAY:

BIBLE VERSE

PSALM 120:1 (*NLT*)

I took my troubles to the Lord; I cried out to him, and he answered my prayer.

REFLECTIONS

People who do not understand will sometimes hastily tell you to get on with your life. They will say you have grieved long enough, and it is time to let go. Please do not give other people power over your grief. *You* decide how long to take because you are the only one who knows your heart, your feelings, and your progress. *You* set the pace. Healing is the goal, so do whatever is necessary to get well. Just take the needed steps to get better.

TODAY:

FEELINGS CHECK
Today I feel:

ONE THING I'M GRATEFUL FOR TODAY:

TODAY'S THOUGHT

No one can do your grieving for you.
Others can stand with you and support you,
but they cannot do it for you.

BIBLE VERSE

ISAIAH 40:28–29 (*NLT*)

Have you never heard or understood? Don't you know that the Lord is the everlasting God, the Creator of all the earth? He never grows faint or weary. No one can measure the depths of his understanding. He gives power to those who are tired and worn out; he offers strength to the weak.

REFLECTIONS

God will give you strength to do the *work* of grieving. Grief is individual and personal. And sometimes grieving feels like a battle. *Fight back* to recover from your grief. *Fight* for your life. Work it out in your own way. You will be glad you did.

TODAY'S THOUGHT

Grief alters your connections to the world, and isolation is unmistakable at times. I felt like a stranger, even to myself, and everything suddenly became a jumbled mess.

TODAY: ______

FEELINGS CHECK
Today I feel:

ONE THING I'M GRATEFUL FOR TODAY:

BIBLE VERSE

JAMES 4:8 (*NLT*)

Draw close to God, and God will draw close to you . . .

REFLECTIONS

Life is uncertain, relationships change, and you may be lonely, but God will not abandon you. He offers stability during chaos. I did not know why I felt isolated after I lost my husband. However, loss alters life and relationships, and everything gets muddled. Consequently, when *unfamiliar* suddenly replaces *familiar,* disconnections occur. With God, you will find consistency and faithfulness. Renewal is there, too.

TODAY:

FEELINGS CHECK
Today I feel:

ONE THING I'M GRATEFUL FOR TODAY:

TODAY'S THOUGHT

Role changes accompany death and loss.
How have your roles changed?

BIBLE VERSE

ECCLESIASTES 3:1 (*NLT*)

There is a time for everything, a season for every activity under heaven.

REFLECTIONS

Change inevitably accompanies death or a major loss. You may have new roles to fulfill, or roles you played before may no longer be necessary. Sometimes new ones are foreign to you, or you may not be ready to step into them without preparation. Adjustments take time, but start somewhere. You may be surprised to find new strengths in yourself. I am certain you can do more than you think.

TODAY'S THOUGHT

Often your purpose for living changes when a loved one dies. Do not allow your life to become a tragedy because of your loss. *Push* yourself to find a new direction, a new passion.

TODAY: ______

FEELINGS CHECK
Today I feel:

ONE THING I'M GRATEFUL FOR TODAY:

BIBLE VERSE

HEBREWS 6:18–19 (*MSG*)

When God wanted to guarantee his promises, he gave his word, a rock-solid guarantee—God can't *break his word. And because his word cannot change, the promise is likewise unchangeable. We who have run for our very lives to God have every reason to grab the promised hope with both hands and never let go. It's an unbreakable spiritual lifeline . . .*

REFLECTIONS

God's purpose for your life is greater than you are—and more than you could *ever* imagine. Discover His purpose that is perfect in every way! He knows you better than you know yourself. Hold fast to the *unbreakable spiritual lifeline* between you and God.

TODAY:

FEELINGS CHECK
Today I feel:

ONE THING I'M GRATEFUL FOR TODAY:

TODAY'S THOUGHT

I will never, ever forget the feelings of utter isolation and loneliness I experienced after my husband died. Describe your most vivid feelings.

BIBLE VERSE

Psalm 40:11 (*MSG*)

Now God, don't hold out on me, don't hold back your passion. Your love and truth are all that keeps me together.

REFLECTIONS

Never before had I suffered the depth of pain I experienced when I lost my husband. I did not even realize it was *possible* to feel such pain, and if ever I needed God, the time was then. You may not realize it, and you may not fully understand now—but hold on to God with all your might! He *is* your lifeline. He *is* your never-ending hope.

TODAY'S THOUGHT

When everything around you is uncertain, you can count on God to remain strong, tireless, unchanging, and reliable.

TODAY: ______

FEELINGS CHECK
Today I feel:

ONE THING I'M GRATEFUL FOR TODAY:

BIBLE VERSE

Hebrews 13:5–6 (*NLT*)

. . . For God has said, "I will never fail you. I will never forsake you." That is why we can say with confidence, "The Lord is my helper, so I will not be afraid. What can mere mortals do to me?"

REFLECTIONS

When life feels confusing, overwhelming, and out of control, you need an anchor of stability and hope. You can *trust* God's promises—and He will not let you down. If you do not know Him, tell Him you *want* to.

TODAY:

FEELINGS CHECK
Today I feel:

ONE THING I'M GRATEFUL FOR TODAY:

REFLECTIONS

God did not create us to live in isolation, and we need other people, especially when times are tough. We *need to know* someone cares. A compassionate look, a heartfelt hug, an understanding word spoken at just the right time . . . the reassurance of someone we trust makes *all the difference.*

TODAY'S THOUGHT

Never underestimate the power of *together*. Don't try to run alone! God's power and the strength of others who understand are immeasurable.

BIBLE VERSE

PROVERBS 27:9 (*NLT*)

The heartfelt counsel of a friend is as sweet as perfume and incense.

TODAY'S THOUGHT

Talking heals. Talking hurts as it heals—but it does heal.

TODAY: ________

FEELINGS CHECK
Today I feel:

ONE THING I'M GRATEFUL FOR TODAY:

BIBLE VERSE

Proverbs 3:5–6 (*MSG*)

Trust God from the bottom of your heart; don't try to figure out everything on your own. Listen for God's voice in everything you do, everywhere you go; he's the one who will keep you on track.

REFLECTIONS

You may have difficulty talking about your feelings or personal matters. Openly sharing with someone may be unnatural for you, but talking about your loss with a person you trust *will bring healing*. Do not be afraid to talk—or, despite your initial discomfort, *go ahead* and talk. You can always cry out to God, at any time, about anything.

TODAY:

FEELINGS CHECK
Today I feel:

ONE THING I'M GRATEFUL FOR TODAY:

TODAY'S THOUGHT

What you do with your grief is up to you. The result depends on how you decide to unpack your experience of loss.

BIBLE VERSE

PSALM 145:18–19 (*NLT*)

The Lord is close to all who call on him, yes, to all who call on him sincerely . . . he hears their cries for help and rescues them.

REFLECTIONS

You are the captain of your grief, and what you do with this potentially life-changing experience is up to you. I hope you will decide to keep facing it—one small step at a time—until you discover renewed passion and new meaning in life. God will help you navigate this course.

TODAY'S THOUGHT

How have your relationships with others changed because of your grief?

TODAY:

FEELINGS CHECK
Today I feel:

ONE THING I'M GRATEFUL FOR TODAY:

BIBLE VERSE

PSALM 23:6 (*NLT*)

Surely your goodness and unfailing love will pursue me all the days of my life . . .

REFLECTIONS

When a relationship unexpectedly changes after a crushing loss, isolation and distress are typical. Slowly, you make adjustments, and some of them are responses to your changing values, priorities, or desires. You also begin to explore new connections as you reestablish your life. Don't forget that God *wants* to help you.

TODAY: ______

FEELINGS CHECK
Today I feel:

ONE THING I'M GRATEFUL FOR TODAY:

TODAY'S THOUGHT

You will probably be shocked to discover how oblivious others can sometimes be toward your loss. If you haven't experienced grief, you cannot know what grief is or how it feels.

BIBLE VERSE

PROVERBS 12:18 (*NIV*)

Reckless words pierce like a sword, but the tongue of the wise brings healing.

REFLECTIONS

If you have not experienced grief firsthand, you *cannot* understand. Sometimes we unrealistically expect too much from others, and we are hurt when they don't act the way we think they should. If they do not understand, how *can* they know how to respond? Try to remember that they probably do not realize they are hurting you. They are just unaware of what you need or how you feel.

TODAY'S THOUGHT

Grievers are often sensitive (or overly sensitive) to words and acts of other people. By learning to let go of these upsetting encounters, a griever helps himself.

TODAY:

FEELINGS CHECK
Today I feel:

ONE THING I'M GRATEFUL FOR TODAY:

BIBLE VERSE

Proverbs 18:19 (*NLT*)

It's harder to make amends with an offended friend than to capture a fortified city. Arguments separate friends like a gate locked with iron bars.

REFLECTIONS

During grief, emotions are already edgy, so a natural impulse is to strike back when someone inadvertently says or does something that hurts. Try to pause and give people a little grace instead of consequences in response to their actions. Realizing they *don't understand* enables you to dismiss hurtful behavior easier—and helps avoid unpleasant confrontations and unwanted results.

TODAY:

FEELINGS CHECK
Today I feel:

ONE THING I'M GRATEFUL FOR TODAY:

TODAY'S THOUGHT

Certain side effects of grief and loss are difficult to understand because they are illogical.

BIBLE VERSE

PSALM 107:27–28 (*MSG*)

You were spun like a top, you reeled like a drunk, you didn't know which end was up. Then you called out to God in your desperate condition; he got you out in the nick of time.

REFLECTIONS

Illogical fears are an unexpected side effect of grief. Certain fears related to grief are understandable, but others make no sense at all. Why did I no longer understand myself? How had I abruptly changed? Why did my husband's death cause my confidence to tumble? Do not let fear overtake you. Fight fear with action. And in your despair, call out to God as the ultimate answer to fear.

TODAY'S THOUGHT

List some actions you are taking to heal. How do you need to change your thinking?

BIBLE VERSE

PROVERBS 20:27 (*NLT*)

The Lord's searchlight penetrates the human spirit, exposing every hidden motive.

TODAY: ________

FEELINGS CHECK
Today I feel:

ONE THING I'M GRATEFUL FOR TODAY:

REFLECTIONS

Resist negative thinking and the downward spiral it triggers. Focus on God instead of your problems, and ask for and accept help when needed. Believe you *will* get well, and replace negative thoughts with positive ones. *Pray*. Shrink the power of the negative by bringing it out into the light and facing it directly and firmly.

TODAY:

FEELINGS CHECK
Today I feel:

ONE THING I'M GRATEFUL FOR TODAY:

REFLECTIONS

Don't let fear paralyze you. Think about it, talk about it, and take action. *Action* is the best antidote for fear, so *move against* your fear.

TODAY'S THOUGHT

Why are you afraid?

BIBLE VERSE

PSALM 91:5–9 (*MSG*)

Fear nothing—not wild wolves in the night, not flying arrows in the day,
Not disease that prowls through the darkness, not disaster that erupts at high noon.
Even though others succumb all around . . . no harm will even graze you.
You'll stand untouched, watch it all from a distance . . . because God's your refuge . . .

TODAY'S THOUGHT

What are your greatest fears?

TODAY:

FEELINGS CHECK
Today I feel:

ONE THING I'M GRATEFUL FOR TODAY:

BIBLE VERSE

PSALM 27:1 (*NLT*)

The Lord is my light and my salvation—so why should I be afraid? The Lord protects me from danger—so why should I tremble?

REFLECTIONS

Fear is common among grievers because the uncertainty of grief generates it. Often, we do not understand what is happening to us, and we don't know what to expect. We may suddenly encounter things we have never faced before. But God *promises* to protect us. In the Bible, God repeatedly tells us *not to be afraid.* He assures us of his presence and help. Trust Him.

TODAY: ____

FEELINGS CHECK
Today I feel:

ONE THING I'M GRATEFUL FOR TODAY:

REFLECTIONS

Defuse your fears by bringing them into the light. Look fear squarely in the face, gather your courage, and take action. Figure out what you can do to counteract your legitimate fears. If you do not know the answers, talk to someone you trust and prepare a plan together. Don't worry about making mistakes because they are simply a way of learning. Mistakes are okay—you will just know to try something different next time.

TODAY'S THOUGHT

Which of your fears are logical? What can you do to alleviate these fears?

BIBLE VERSE

II Chronicles 20:15 (*NLT*)

. . . This is what the Lord says: Do not be afraid! Don't be discouraged . . . for the battle is not yours, but God's.

TODAY'S THOUGHT

What do you need, and whose advice do you trust? Ask for help . . .

BIBLE VERSE

PROVERBS 12:15 (*MSG*)

Fools are headstrong and do what they like; wise people take advice.

TODAY:

FEELINGS CHECK
Today I feel:

ONE THING I'M GRATEFUL FOR TODAY:

REFLECTIONS

Grief confuses thinking, especially early on, so your judgment may not be as sharp as usual. Someone else may have a clearer, more objective point of view and be in a better position to suggest alternatives. Ask—and then listen. Getting advice when you need it is a wise decision.

TODAY:

FEELINGS CHECK
Today I feel:

ONE THING I'M GRATEFUL FOR TODAY:

TODAY'S THOUGHT

Life is continually changing. How do you react to change?

BIBLE VERSE

ROMANS 8:31–32 (*MSG*)

So, what do you think? With God on our side like this, how can we lose? If God didn't hesitate to put everything on the line for us, embracing our condition and exposing himself to the worst by sending his own Son, is there anything else he wouldn't gladly and freely do for us?

REFLECTIONS

Have unexpected changes overwhelmed you? Everything in your life may be unsettled and confusing, but God is always the same! Change is inevitable, but it is not struggle-free. God did not hesitate for an instant to put *everything,* including His Son's life, on the line for us. He proved He would go to any lengths to secure our best because He loves us. Let Him help you with the difficult adjustments. He is a solid rock—trustworthy and constant.

TODAY'S THOUGHT

You can make it through grief, but not by yourself. Whose help will you accept?

TODAY: ______

FEELINGS CHECK
Today I feel:

ONE THING I'M GRATEFUL FOR TODAY:

BIBLE VERSE

ECCLESIASTES 4:12 (*MSG*)

By yourself you're unprotected. With a friend you can face the worst . . .

REFLECTIONS

Allow other people to help you. We were not designed to work out our grief alone—we *need* each other and we *need* God. We can make it, but not by ourselves. Grief is too hard to successfully face alone. And why would you want to try?

TODAY: ______

FEELINGS CHECK
Today I feel:

ONE THING I'M GRATEFUL FOR TODAY:

REFLECTIONS

A mistake is not final—it is just a lesson learned! If you are making mistakes, it means you're *trying*, you are *taking action*. You are *not paralyzed by fear*. This is a good thing!

TODAY'S THOUGHT

A mistake is not a failure—it's just a valuable lesson about how not to do something. What do you need to try in a different way?

BIBLE VERSE

Psalm 37:24 (*MSG*)

If he stumbles, he's not down for long; God has a grip on his hand.

TODAY'S THOUGHT

Fear shrinks when exposed to the light. What will you bring into the light today?

TODAY: ________

FEELINGS CHECK
Today I feel:

ONE THING I'M GRATEFUL FOR TODAY:

BIBLE VERSE

EPHESIANS 5:13–14 (*GOD'S WORD*)

Light exposes the true character of everything because light makes everything easy to see . . .

REFLECTIONS

Look fear in the face. Bring it into the light, and suddenly it's not as scary as you first thought. In the light, you can identify what is creating your fear, and its power over you diminishes. Talk about it, pray about it, move against it—and you, instead of the fear, will be in control.

TODAY:

FEELINGS CHECK
Today I feel:

ONE THING I'M GRATEFUL FOR TODAY:

TODAY'S THOUGHT

You may not be able to do as much as you would like, or as much as you think you *should,* but you can always do something. You *can* do *something* . . .

BIBLE VERSE

PROVERBS 28:20 (*MSG*)

Committed and persistent work pays off . . .

REFLECTIONS

Take action. Do something. Once you *start* moving, it is easier to *keep moving* forward. Inevitably, as you see positive results, your optimism will grow. So start doing something.

TODAY'S THOUGHT

What do you need to
find the courage to do?

TODAY: ______

FEELINGS CHECK
Today I feel:

______

______

BIBLE VERSE

Joshua 1:9 (*NLT*)

. . . *"Do not be afraid or discouraged. For the Lord your God is with you wherever you go."*

ONE THING I'M GRATEFUL FOR TODAY:

______

______

______

REFLECTIONS

Courage is not the absence of fear—it's *doing* what you're *afraid* to do. What do you need to do? Take the first step, and the others will get easier.

TODAY: ________

FEELINGS CHECK
Today I feel:

ONE THING I'M GRATEFUL FOR TODAY:

TODAY'S THOUGHT

Do you really want to get well? Your answer to this question is vital.

BIBLE VERSE

PSALM 6:6–7 (*NLT*)

I am worn out from sobbing. Every night tears drench my bed; my pillow is wet from weeping. My vision is blurred by grief . . .

REFLECTIONS

Desire to get well is essential, and your thoughts and actions *do* make a difference. Grief is an active process. You are in control, and you make the decisions about *what you will do* to get better. I wish you could change what has happened, but you can't. And while you cannot change other people, you *can* make personal changes to get better. Grief is devastating—and though it is a natural place to be after a loss, you do not want to make your home there.

TODAY'S THOUGHT

Victor or victim? It's a choice you make every day.

TODAY: ________

FEELINGS CHECK
Today I feel:

ONE THING I'M GRATEFUL FOR TODAY:

BIBLE VERSE

II Corinthians 12:9 (*MSG*)

. . . and then he [God] told me, "My grace is enough; it's all you need. My strength comes into its own in your weakness."

REFLECTIONS

Will you be a victor or a victim? You choose your attitude and control your resolve to heal *each day*. God can give you the strength to do what you need to do. Decide every day to be a victor! Do not be deceived—a proactive attitude has *everything* to do with healing.

TODAY:

FEELINGS CHECK
Today I feel:

ONE THING I'M GRATEFUL FOR TODAY:

TODAY'S THOUGHT

Fight off any tendency toward blame or bitterness over your loss, and focus instead on the blessings you still have.

BIBLE VERSE

HEBREWS 12:15 (*MSG*)

. . . Keep a sharp eye out for weeds of bitter discontent. A thistle or two gone to seed can ruin a whole garden in no time.

REFLECTIONS

Don't let yourself become trapped by feelings of bitterness or blame over your loss. I would be lying if I said those feelings never entered my mind; in times of weakness and fatigue, they did. However, pledge to yourself that you will not allow bitterness *to live* in your heart. Replace blame and resentment with gratitude to God for all that you still have, and you will open yourself to His healing.

TODAY'S THOUGHT

Tragedy will test you like nothing else. But when you commit to act (along with God's help), you *will* rise above it in spite of your pain—and see a new beginning.

TODAY: ______

FEELINGS CHECK
Today I feel:

ONE THING I'M GRATEFUL FOR TODAY:

BIBLE VERSE

PSALM 147:3 (*MSG*)

He heals the heartbroken and bandages their wounds.

REFLECTIONS

God will always be faithful, and you never have to wrestle with whether or not He will listen when you call. Tragedy tests you unlike *anything* else, but with God's help, you have the power to rise above it, work through it, and find a new beginning. Be encouraged, do not quit, take action, and God will be true to His promises.

TODAY:

FEELINGS CHECK
Today I feel:

ONE THING I'M GRATEFUL FOR TODAY:

REFLECTIONS

During personal struggle, worry is a pitfall waiting to snag you. We do not understand what is happening after a loss, we see no end in sight, and we don't know what to do—so we fret. But God tells us to pray instead. If you do not already know God's promises, I hope you will search for them and allow God to help. His power is inconceivable, and He will not disappoint you. Watch what happens.

TODAY'S THOUGHT

Everything inside and outside of oneself is out of balance and off-course—and time seems to come to a screeching halt.

BIBLE VERSE

PHILIPPIANS 4:6–7 (*MSG*)

Don't fret or worry. Instead of worrying, pray. Let petitions and praises shape your worries into prayers, letting God know your concerns. Before you know it, a sense of God's wholeness, everything coming together for good, will come and settle you down . . .

TODAY'S THOUGHT

Anything can suddenly trigger a reminder of your loss.

TODAY: ________

FEELINGS CHECK
Today I feel:

ONE THING I'M GRATEFUL FOR TODAY:

BIBLE VERSE

PSALM 41:12 (*MSG*)

You [God] know me inside and out, you hold me together . . .

REFLECTIONS

A song, a place, a photo, a memory, something someone says—can all trigger a reminder of your loss. Accept the reminders (and the tears) and keep moving forward. As time passes, the reminders will be less frequent and less intense, and they will become precious memories instead of sharp pains.

TODAY:

FEELINGS CHECK
Today I feel:

ONE THING I'M GRATEFUL FOR TODAY:

TODAY'S THOUGHT

Grief is not a passive process. And time, by itself, has nothing to do with healing.

BIBLE VERSE

Romans 5:3–4 (*God's Word*)

. . . We know that suffering creates endurance, endurance creates character, and character creates confidence.

REFLECTIONS

Working through grief requires action. Pain does not go away just because a certain amount of time has passed, but w*hat you do* with the time is crucial. While you would not choose to endure the pain of grief, suffering does produce growth. You *will* grow because of what you have been through, but the way you grow depends on you.

TODAY'S THOUGHT

You must *experience* the pain of your loss for healing to occur.

TODAY:

FEELINGS CHECK
Today I feel:

ONE THING I'M GRATEFUL FOR TODAY:

BIBLE VERSE

PSALM 119:28–29 (*NLT*)

I weep with grief; encourage me by your word. Keep me from lying to myself . . .

REFLECTIONS

Healing will not take place unless you *feel* the pain. Confronting the pain and working through it *will* bring healthy resolution to your grief. And then, in time, you'll be able to let go of the past, embrace life, and look toward the future again. You have to go *full circle* through the grief—to reach the other side.

TODAY:

FEELINGS CHECK
Today I feel:

ONE THING I'M GRATEFUL FOR TODAY:

TODAY'S THOUGHT

Do you sometimes feel as though you're going crazy? Talk to someone who is grieving . . . and you will likely find that she feels the same way for a time.

BIBLE VERSE

PROVERBS 9:4, 6 (*MSG*)

"Are you confused about life, don't know what's going on? Come with me, oh come . . .

Leave your impoverished confusion and live!" . . .

REFLECTIONS

I do not think I have talked to any grievers who have not questioned, at some point, if they were going crazy. When you are in emotional, relational, physical, spiritual, and intellectual turmoil—is it any surprise that you might wonder if your reactions are normal? Most likely they are, but it's reassuring to learn what to expect and know that others have felt the same way.

TODAY'S THOUGHT

Do you sometimes think God has forgotten about you? Or do you mistakenly think you're being punished?

TODAY: ____________

FEELINGS CHECK
Today I feel:

ONE THING I'M GRATEFUL FOR TODAY:

BIBLE VERSE

EPHESIANS 3:18–19 (*NLT*)

And may you have the power to understand, as all God's people should, how wide, how long, how high, and how deep his love really is. May you experience the love of Christ, though it is so great you will never fully understand it. Then you will be filled with the fullness of life and power that comes from God.

REFLECTIONS

When you focus on your pain, time stands still—and it *seems* as though the pain will never end. When your eyes focus inward, you may feel as though God has forgotten you and He's not paying attention. When tragic things happen, you may wonder what you have done to deserve the hardship. But God's love is unquestionable, and you are *not* being punished. Trust God's promises and His character.

TODAY:

FEELINGS CHECK
Today I feel:

ONE THING I'M GRATEFUL FOR TODAY:

TODAY'S THOUGHT

Grief, in its early stages, is an inward look that is so intense—it is hard to see or think about anything else.

BIBLE VERSE

JOB 30:27 (*MSG*)

My stomach's in a constant churning, never settles down. Each day confronts me with more suffering.

REFLECTIONS

This verse may well describe the way you felt during the early stages of grief. Thankfully, you will not remain there. The agonizing pain of losing someone you love dearly is nearly indescribable. But let me reassure you there is a path through grief—and you *will* find healing if you follow the path and take the needed steps to bring acceptance, release, and renewal.

TODAY'S THOUGHT

You may be alarmed by the intensity of your emotions—or by your *out-of-character* responses.

TODAY:

FEELINGS CHECK
Today I feel:

ONE THING I'M GRATEFUL FOR TODAY:

BIBLE VERSE

PSALM 55:7–8 (*MSG*)

Get me out of here on dove wings; I want some peace and quiet. I want a walk in the country, I want a cabin in the woods. I'm desperate for a change from rage and stormy weather.

REFLECTIONS

I was on an emotional roller coaster, and the intensity of my feelings startled me. Generally calm and peaceful, I realized that certain circumstances and words spoken by others triggered anger, hostility, and moodiness in me. My responses were needlessly sharp. Unexpected feelings and reactions concerned me, and I changed my behavior after other people confronted me about it. Later, these responses faded.

TODAY:

FEELINGS CHECK
Today I feel:

ONE THING I'M GRATEFUL FOR TODAY:

TODAY'S THOUGHT

I would not have survived grief without God's presence because many times, I did not even want to. God *will* bring you through, and He never leaves you.

BIBLE VERSE

Psalm 121:3, 8 (*NLT*)

He will not let you stumble and fall; the one who watches over you will not sleep.

The Lord keeps watch over you as you come and go, both now and forever.

REFLECTIONS

During the depths of grief, at times I did not want to go on. Thankfully, I kept going for my daughter's sake when I could not do it for myself. Without God's ever-present help, I am convinced I never would have made it. He watches over you *constantly, tirelessly, and lovingly.* Accept His power and presence in your life. Look to Him. He wants to meet your needs.

TODAY'S THOUGHT

Practical support is available in books, grief-support groups, journaling, talking with a friend, and counseling. Find the right kind of help for you.

TODAY: ______

FEELINGS CHECK
Today I feel:

ONE THING I'M GRATEFUL FOR TODAY:

BIBLE VERSE

PROVERBS 23:12 (*NLT*)

Commit yourself to instruction; attune your ears to hear words of knowledge.

REFLECTIONS

Help is accessible in many forms. I *had* to figure out what was happening to me because the symptoms were completely unsettling. I started reading books about grief to find out what was normal and what to expect, and joined a grief-support group. Some people may be more comfortable with a counselor than a group, and others may need both. Journaling is an effective supplement to anything else you do. Find the help that fits you and make use of it. But don't try to do this alone!

TODAY: ______

FEELINGS CHECK
Today I feel:

ONE THING I'M GRATEFUL FOR TODAY:

REFLECTIONS

We *need* to have our grief feelings validated by others. We need to know, *really know*, that someone cares. Grief is one of the most gut-wrenching experiences you will face in life, and you want to know you are not alone. Sometimes words are unnecessary—but you need someone to hold you tightly while you cry, to touch your hand, and to look deeply into your eyes. You need to *see and feel* his compassion. You need the connection of another person.

TODAY'S THOUGHT

Sometimes words are unimportant. We just need to *connect* with others and allow them to connect with us. Empathy, direct eye contact, and the touch of another human being speak volumes.

BIBLE VERSE

I CORINTHIANS 13:4–5 (*MSG*)

Love never gives up. Love cares more for others than for self. . . Doesn't force itself on others . . . Doesn't fly off the handle . . .

TODAY'S THOUGHT

When we hurt we tend to withdraw, and grief presses us toward isolation. But to heal completely, we need to share our grief with others.

TODAY: ________

FEELINGS CHECK
Today I feel:

ONE THING I'M GRATEFUL FOR TODAY:

BIBLE VERSE

GALATIANS 6:2 (*NLT*)

Share each other's troubles and problems . . .

REFLECTIONS

The pain of grief *sways* us to isolate ourselves unless we fight against our natural urges to withdraw. If we build walls and try to keep people away whenever we are in pain, our lives will be dismal. And unless we find a way to release the pain, our bodies will eventually suffer the consequences. Sharing your grief promotes complete healing. Connect with others and allow them to connect with you—it's the way to get well.

TODAY:

FEELINGS CHECK
Today I feel:

ONE THING I'M GRATEFUL FOR TODAY:

TODAY'S THOUGHT

The only effective way to face grief is head-on.

BIBLE VERSE

Jeremiah 6:14 (*TLB*)

You can't heal a wound by saying it's not there!

REFLECTIONS

I remember hearing a statement at the first grief-support group I attended: "You can't go over, under, or around grief—you must walk straight through it." Avoiding pain is a natural tendency; however, unless we feel the pain, we cannot heal. *Break through* the darkness . . . and see sunlight again.

TODAY'S THOUGHT

What are the biggest adjustments and challenges you have faced so far because of your loss?

BIBLE VERSE

Proverbs 2:3–4 (*NLT*)

Cry out for insight and understanding. Search for them as you would for lost money or hidden treasure.

TODAY: ______

FEELINGS CHECK
Today I feel:

ONE THING I'M GRATEFUL FOR TODAY:

REFLECTIONS

One of my biggest challenges was accepting that I was no longer part of a couple. My husband and I shared all areas of our lives—decisions, finances, social activities, family, spiritual ties, household tasks, and on and on. We supported each other. I had never seriously considered being alone, and was shocked and devastated when it happened. I had much to learn and many adjustments to make.

TODAY:

FEELINGS CHECK
Today I feel:

ONE THING I'M GRATEFUL FOR TODAY:

TODAY'S THOUGHT

While we have no choice as to most of the obstacles we face, we do get to choose our responses to these challenges. And our responses determine the outcome.

BIBLE VERSE

Isaiah 46:3–4 (*NLT*)

Listen to me . . . I created you and have cared for you since before you were born. I will be your God throughout your lifetime—until your hair is white with age. I made you, and I will care for you. I will carry you along and save you.

REFLECTIONS

Each of us faces tragedies and difficulties throughout life, and the way we *choose* to respond shapes the rest of our lives. Will you respond positively or negatively, in faith or in fear? Will your choice be a bridge or a roadblock? Will the tragedy bring growth or pigeonhole you in an unhealthy place? Do not allow your loss to become the greatest tragedy in your life. Let God bring something good out of your pain.

TODAY'S THOUGHT

As children of God, we are far more powerful than we sometimes realize. A Christian has access to the ultimate power of all—the Holy Spirit. Remember what He can do.

TODAY: ________

FEELINGS CHECK
Today I feel:

ONE THING I'M GRATEFUL FOR TODAY:

BIBLE VERSE

EPHESIANS 3:20 (*MSG*)

God can do anything, you know—far more than you could ever imagine or guess or request in your wildest dreams! He does it not by pushing us around but by working within us, his Spirit deeply and gently within us.

REFLECTIONS

When we join God's family, we have the power of the Holy Spirit living *within* us—the ultimate power of the entire universe! The power of God that created the world, raised the dead, and created people is alive, well, and working within us as Christians! God wants to guide us, to help us, and to lead us into His best. Talk to Him and listen to Him. He will not fail you.

TODAY:

FEELINGS CHECK
Today I feel:

ONE THING I'M GRATEFUL FOR TODAY:

TODAY'S THOUGHT

Many times, we want to give up. But if we hang on, at some point, the life vision, the "dreams" resurface—and we *make the decision* to live again.

BIBLE VERSE

ROMANS 15:13 (*MSG*)

Oh! May the God of green hope fill you up with joy, fill you up with peace, so that your believing lives, filled with the life-giving energy of the Holy Spirit, will brim over with hope!

REFLECTIONS

Grief is work, and often we have to *remind* ourselves to keep going because we feel like giving up. However, if you hang on and keep moving, you will reach a turning point—when you decide to live again! People often remember exactly when they made this pivotal decision because life wins out over death. Keep going until your dreams resurface. Listen to the deep longings of your heart and follow wherever they lead. Get back into the sea of life.

TODAY'S THOUGHT

Initially, a dream may be only a shadow, a spark of what's to come . . . but it's conceived out of *something* resonating deep within your soul and calling you *to live*. Listen.

TODAY:

FEELINGS CHECK
Today I feel:

ONE THING I'M GRATEFUL FOR TODAY:

BIBLE VERSE

ISAIAH 58:11 (*NLT*)

The Lord will guide you continually, watering your life when you are dry and keeping you healthy, too. You will be like a well-watered garden, like an ever-flowing spring.

REFLECTIONS

Listen to your heart. What subject keeps returning to your mind? What excites you? What do you long to achieve? What do you love to do or be around? Whom do you want to help? *What stirs your heart?* Dare to step out, in spite of your fear, and follow your heart. Take chances. Live again!

TODAY:

FEELINGS CHECK
Today I feel:

ONE THING I'M GRATEFUL FOR TODAY:

TODAY'S THOUGHT

If you were not afraid of failing,
what would you love to try?

BIBLE VERSE

PSALM 37:5 (*NLT*)

Commit everything you do to the Lord. Trust him, and he will help you.

REFLECTIONS

A dream changes form and direction as you go—inspiring you to risk doing something worthwhile, to look for the best fruit at the end of the skinny branches, and to go where you are afraid to go. Follow your heart, in spite of fear, self-doubt, or procrastination. Get out of the safe harbor of your comfort zone and take chances. With God's help, *make the decision to live again*. He wants your life to be all it can be!

TODAY'S THOUGHT

Grief is tumultuous, unpredictable, and ever-changing. Feelings and reactions hover just below the surface and when provoked, they sometimes ambush us. Learn to treat yourself *gently*.

TODAY: ______

FEELINGS CHECK
Today I feel:

______

______

ONE THING I'M GRATEFUL FOR TODAY:

______

______

______

BIBLE VERSE

MATTHEW 11:28–30 (*MSG*)

"Are you tired? Worn out? Burned out on religion? Come to me. Get away with me and you'll recover your life. I'll show you how to take a real rest. Walk with me and work with me—watch how I do it. Learn the unforced rhythms of grace . . . Keep company with me and you'll learn to live freely and lightly."

REFLECTIONS

The path of grief is bumpy and the obstacles are challenging. Ups and downs take you by surprise, again and again, but if you understand the nature of grief, you'll be better prepared for the disorderly process. The back-and-forth path is normal, and while you may *feel* you are regressing, you are not—this is simply the way of grief. Be gentle with yourself! You *are* getting better.

TODAY:

FEELINGS CHECK
Today I feel:

ONE THING
I'M GRATEFUL
FOR TODAY:

TODAY'S THOUGHT

Learning what to expect can free you to experience the process and stop beating yourself up when you get knocked down.

BIBLE VERSE

PROVERBS 16:25 (*NCV*™)

Patience is better than strength. Controlling your temper is better than capturing a city.

REFLECTIONS

Once you realize the up-and-down, back-and-forth nature of grief, you will know what to expect and will not be surprised if you suddenly take a spill. When you understand grief's reality, you are free to experience it, work through the pain, and see past it. Stop and remember not to beat yourself up because you thought you were farther along. In fact, you *are* making progress! Be patient. Grieving takes time. It's *a process*.

TODAY'S THOUGHT

Sometimes you have to struggle to gain control over your emotions or they will rule your life.

TODAY: _______

FEELINGS CHECK
Today I feel:

ONE THING I'M GRATEFUL FOR TODAY:

BIBLE VERSE

Psalm 37:8 (*NCV*™)

Don't get angry. Don't be upset; it only leads to trouble.

Proverbs 10:17 (*MSG*)

The road to life is a disciplined life . . .

REFLECTIONS

Since emotions are already in high gear during grief, unless you rein them in and take control, they will rule your life. Counteract an emotion by taking an opposite action, and *act* your way into a feeling until the feeling becomes reality. For example, do something in spite of your fear, or laugh when you do not feel happy. By doing this, you can begin to change the way you feel instead of giving in to negative emotions. Try it.

TODAY:

FEELINGS CHECK
Today I feel:

ONE THING I'M GRATEFUL FOR TODAY:

TODAY'S THOUGHT

What are some of the "bumps" (or challenges) you have encountered? How have you handled them?

BIBLE VERSE

II Corinthians 4:8–9 (*NLT*)

We are pressed on every side by troubles, but we are not crushed and broken. We are perplexed, but we don't give up and quit. We are hunted down, but God never abandons us. We get knocked down, but we get up again and keep going.

REFLECTIONS

No doubt, grief has brought challenges into your life. Have you struggled with relationships, finances, emotions, isolation, insensitivity of other people, or depression? Or perhaps you have wrestled with something else. Face your challenges from the mindset of a victor. Assume a positive stance and take action—because you will get well faster if you do. Keep moving forward, one step at a time.

TODAY'S THOUGHT

Anger is common among grievers—at certain points during grief. Sometimes anger can even help us decide "Enough is enough,"—and then we'll do whatever is necessary to get better.

BIBLE VERSE

PROVERBS 25:28 (*MSG*)

A person without self-control is like a house with its doors and windows knocked out.

TODAY: ______

FEELINGS CHECK
Today I feel:

ONE THING I'M GRATEFUL FOR TODAY:

REFLECTIONS

Anger is normal when working through grief unless it lingers too long or harms others. Anger can be *helpful* if it spurs us to decide it is time to take the necessary steps to get better. Anger reminds us, after feeling numb, that our emotions are reawakening and we are still alive. Let anger serve a positive purpose in your grief and propel you toward healing.

TODAY: ______

FEELINGS CHECK
Today I feel:

ONE THING I'M GRATEFUL FOR TODAY:

REFLECTIONS

Anger at God can be difficult to face. While anger is a normal response to loss, do not hold on to anger and allow it to dominate your thoughts and actions. Constructively resolving these feelings, and all the emotions connected to grief, brings healing.

TODAY'S THOUGHT

Anger toward God can generate tremendous guilt feelings.

BIBLE VERSE

Ephesians 4:26–27 (*MSG*)

Go ahead and be angry. You do well to be angry—but don't use your anger as fuel for revenge. And don't stay angry. Don't go to bed angry. Don't give the Devil that kind of foothold in your life.

TODAY'S THOUGHT

Guilt is one of Satan's most powerful tools of deception. *Remind* yourself that we can never drift too far from God's love and grace.

TODAY: ______

FEELINGS CHECK
Today I feel:

ONE THING I'M GRATEFUL FOR TODAY:

BIBLE VERSE

JOHN 6:37 (*GOD'S WORD*)

. . . I will never turn away anyone who comes to me.

II CORINTHIANS 11:14 (*MSG*)

Satan does it all the time, dressing up as a beautiful angel of light.

REFLECTIONS

Satan is a powerful deceiver and relentless pursuer of anyone who seeks God. He will try to turn you away from God through guilt, doubt, shame, confusion, busyness, anger, frustration, distraction, rejection, disappointment, or any way he can. Do not let him convince you that you've fallen hopelessly away from God's love and grace with no way of return. Trust God's assurance that He will never turn away anyone who comes to Him—and then tell Satan to flee!

TODAY: ______

FEELINGS CHECK
Today I feel:

ONE THING I'M GRATEFUL FOR TODAY:

TODAY'S THOUGHT

Forgiving others is difficult, but necessary. Unforgiveness will not only hurt us, but will keep us from being in a right relationship with God. Forgiveness is a *decision*—not a feeling.

BIBLE VERSE

LUKE 6:37 (*NLT*)

Stop judging others, and you will not be judged. Stop criticizing others, or it will all come back on you. If you forgive others, you will be forgiven.

REFLECTIONS

Forgiveness is not optional—it is a *command* from God. And forgiveness is not a feeling, but a *decision* and an *action*. The Bible teaches that if we do not forgive others, God will not forgive us. Unforgiveness destroys a heart as surely as disease destroys a body. Forgiveness is essential to healing and to a right relationship with God. Don't wait—take the necessary steps today.

TODAY'S THOUGHT

Forgiveness releases a *legitimate* debt that *cannot be repaid.* Forgiveness sets the prisoner free—and the prisoner is you.

TODAY: ______

FEELINGS CHECK
Today I feel:

ONE THING I'M GRATEFUL FOR TODAY:

BIBLE VERSE

LUKE 17:4 (*NLT*)

"Even if he wrongs you seven times a day and each time turns again and asks forgiveness, forgive him."

REFLECTIONS

Unforgiveness is a trap (and a lie) that destroys hearts and separates us from God. We harm *ourselves* by unforgiveness, and by hanging on to a rightful debt that cannot be repaid, we make ourselves prisoners. By forgiving, we release the debt owed to us. And in turn, we release ourselves from its hold over us, opening the door to healing with God and others.

TODAY:

FEELINGS CHECK
Today I feel:

ONE THING I'M GRATEFUL FOR TODAY:

REFLECTIONS

Circumstances surrounding death or loss may generate 'Why?' questions, but 'Why?' questions can snowball and become a stumbling block. I respectfully suggest that the *why* is not important. If you knew why, would you grieve less? Would anything change? Would knowing why make any difference? *Questioning* is a normal response to loss, but being trapped there will obstruct healing.

TODAY'S THOUGHT

Some people get so wrapped up in "Why?" questions that they can't get beyond this point. If you knew why, would you grieve less?

BIBLE VERSE

PSALM 27:8 (*NLT*)

My heart has heard you say, "Come and talk with me." And my heart responds, "Lord, I am coming."

TODAY'S THOUGHT

Are you trusting God? Will He take care of you or not?

TODAY: ______

FEELINGS CHECK
Today I feel:

ONE THING I'M GRATEFUL FOR TODAY:

BIBLE VERSE

PSALM 28:6–7 (*MSG*)

Blessed be God—he heard me praying. He proved he's on my side; I've thrown my lot in with him. Now I'm jumping for joy, and shouting and singing my thanks to him.

REFLECTIONS

Faith and trust are the bottom line. God is in complete control, and while some events are not His will, He is aware of *everything* that happens. Perhaps asking God what He wants to *teach* us from our situations rather than why we are there is a healthier action. He promises to be present through all of our circumstances, and nothing can separate us from His love. He is able to bring good out of anything we face. Will you trust in His provision, character, and strength?

TODAY:

FEELINGS CHECK
Today I feel:

ONE THING I'M GRATEFUL FOR TODAY:

TODAY'S THOUGHT

Surrender is necessary for healing, but surrender does not mean forgetting the person or the past. "Letting go" signals acceptance of your loss. Describe how you are beginning to surrender.

BIBLE VERSE

NAHUM 1:7 (*NLT*)

The Lord is good. When trouble comes, he is a strong refuge. And he knows everyone who trusts in him.

REFLECTIONS

Sometimes grievers misunderstand what surrender means and think they have to forget their loved ones. Instead, surrender means you are beginning to accept your loss and focus your attention on reinvesting in the future. You are starting to think about living again. Setbacks will occur, but your awareness of the future begins to replace an overall preoccupation with your loss. You are moving forward.

TODAY'S THOUGHT

If you are still alive, God has a purpose for your being here. His purpose is perfect, and He knows you better than you know yourself.

TODAY: ______

FEELINGS CHECK
Today I feel:

ONE THING I'M GRATEFUL FOR TODAY:

BIBLE VERSE

Exodus 9:16 (*NIV*)

But I have raised you up for this very purpose, that I might show you my power and that my name might be proclaimed in all the earth.

REFLECTIONS

You can be certain that if you are still alive, you're here for a reason. God created you for his purposes—as part of His intricate plan. As long as He has plans that you are instrumental in carrying out, your life on earth will continue. You can trust that He knows you better than you know yourself, and His objectives are greater (and more creative) than anything you could devise. Tune in and discover what He has designed for you.

TODAY:

FEELINGS CHECK
Today I feel:

ONE THING I'M GRATEFUL FOR TODAY:

REFLECTIONS

Anger, guilt, depression, and "Why?" questions are common early responses to grief and loss, but do not let yourself get stuck there. While feelings are non-negotiable, and denying them is unhealthy, respond in a way that leads to healing. Examining *how* you feel and *why*—and *working through* your feelings—is the healthy path to take. What do you need to do?

TODAY'S THOUGHT

Describe your struggles with anger, guilt, depression, and "Why?" questions. If you still need to forgive someone, talk about it.

BIBLE VERSE

MATTHEW 6:14–15 (*MSG*)

"In prayer there is a connection between what God does and what you do. You can't get forgiveness from God, for instance, without also forgiving others. If you refuse to do your part, you cut yourself off from God's part."

TODAY'S THOUGHT

Using your emotions to gauge the reliability of *anything*, particularly spiritual issues, is unwise.

TODAY: ______

FEELINGS CHECK
Today I feel:

ONE THING I'M GRATEFUL FOR TODAY:

BIBLE VERSE

PSALM 61:2 (*NLT*)

From the ends of the earth, I will cry to you for help, for my heart is overwhelmed. Lead me to the towering rock of safety, for you are my safe refuge . . .

REFLECTIONS

Feelings are an unreliable decision-making tool. Grief spirals emotions into high gear, creating doubt and confusion. Sometimes things are not as they *seem*. God is with you even when you do not *feel* His presence. He is *always* working on your behalf, whether or not His actions are visible. Focus on spiritual truths and affirm the promises of God through His Word. If you do, you will be standing on solid ground.

TODAY: ______

FEELINGS CHECK
Today I feel:

ONE THING I'M GRATEFUL FOR TODAY:

TODAY'S THOUGHT

Sometimes we impulsively make decisions, hoping the change will make us feel better and lessen our pain. However, when possible, delay major decisions during grief.

BIBLE VERSE

PROVERBS 19:2 (*NLT*)

Zeal without knowledge is not good; a person who moves too quickly may go the wrong way.

REFLECTIONS

At times, escape *appears* to be a preferable alternative to facing a painful or difficult situation. However, escape will only delay the pain, not heal it. Making decisions too quickly or without consideration can create avoidable problems. Grief affects concentration, so others' perceptions may be more thorough and objective than your own. Stop, think, and ask trusted people for advice. Carefully weigh the options before making major decisions.

TODAY'S THOUGHT

Numerous losses at one time add extra dimension to an already difficult grief journey. Are you experiencing more than one loss?

TODAY: ______

FEELINGS CHECK
Today I feel:

ONE THING I'M GRATEFUL FOR TODAY:

BIBLE VERSE

John 16:33 (*NLT*)

"I have told you all this so that you may have peace in me. Here on earth you will have many trials and sorrows. But take heart, because I have overcome the world."

REFLECTIONS

When you face several losses at once, grief intensifies. You may be in this situation and fail to grasp the significance of being bombarded by a number of anxieties, adjustments, and sorrows. Examine your losses and *be gentle with yourself. Even more* may be going on than you realize . . . so be aware.

TODAY:

FEELINGS CHECK
Today I feel:

ONE THING I'M GRATEFUL FOR TODAY:

TODAY'S THOUGHT

What are you doing to keep your emotions in check while still working through them? How are you dealing with decisions particularly affected by your emotions?

BIBLE VERSE

II Timothy 1:7 (*NLT*)

For God has not given us a spirit of fear and timidity, but of power, love, and self-discipline.

REFLECTIONS

Emotions will rule your life and create havoc unless you take control. *Consciously act* to counteract the negative. Challenge erroneous emotional messages by reminding yourself of God's truth. Stop ruminating over *anything* that threatens to send you into a downward spiral. Regain control by reading scripture verses or repeating affirmations aloud. Or get feedback from a reliable friend. Use whatever works—but *seize control* of your emotions so they do not control you.

TODAY'S THOUGHT

Your thoughts are critical. They can be a friend or an enemy—and *you* decide what to think about. Your thoughts determine who you are and what you do.

TODAY: ______

FEELINGS CHECK
Today I feel:

ONE THING I'M GRATEFUL FOR TODAY:

BIBLE VERSE

HEBREWS 4:12 (*NLT*)

For the word of God is full of living power. It is sharper than the sharpest knife, cutting deep into our innermost thoughts and desires. It exposes us for what we really are.

REFLECTIONS

Your thoughts determine your life, and you *choose* what to contemplate. While you are not responsible for every thought that flashes into your head, you are accountable for the ones you allow to settle there. Positive or negative, your thoughts propel you down a path, so make sure it's the path you want. God is always ready to help, but we are responsible for our decisions and actions.

TODAY:

FEELINGS CHECK
Today I feel:

ONE THING I'M GRATEFUL FOR TODAY:

TODAY'S THOUGHT

Your attitudes determine the substance, direction, and quality of your life. Are you a positive or a negative magnet?

BIBLE VERSE

PROVERBS 23:7 (*NKJV*™)

For as he thinks in his heart, so is he.

REFLECTIONS

Your thoughts act like a magnet to draw those same things into your life (positive or negative people, experiences, and ways of thinking). So ultimately, your thoughts and their results drive the quality of your life. Monitor your thoughts. Focus on positive ideas if you want to live a positive life, and on faith instead of fear. Dwell on power rather than weakness. Consciously *direct* your thoughts.

TODAY'S THOUGHT

What we *think* about our circumstances makes all the difference in the world.

TODAY: ______

FEELINGS CHECK
Today I feel:

ONE THING I'M GRATEFUL FOR TODAY:

BIBLE VERSE

PHILIPPIANS 2:5 (*NLT*)

Your attitude should be the same that Christ Jesus had.

REFLECTIONS

When you consider things from Jesus' point of view, you will never go wrong. His thinking never defeated him. Thoughts become a self-fulfilling prophecy, so when you focus on fear, fear will escalate; focus on faith and faith will strengthen. *How you approach* your circumstances makes things better or worse, so why make things worse? Why does the same situation bring success to one person and defeat to another? Your attitude triggers the difference.

TODAY:

FEELINGS CHECK
Today I feel:

ONE THING I'M GRATEFUL FOR TODAY:

TODAY'S THOUGHT

When we align ourselves with God's will, focus on His thoughts and promises, and submit to His commands, we activate His power and blessings in our lives. We open up the pipeline!

BIBLE VERSE

PHILIPPIANS 2:13 (*NLT*)

For God is working in you, giving you the desire to obey him and the power to do what pleases him.

REFLECTIONS

God *wants* to demonstrate his power through us, but He will never force His will on us. He is not an intruder. And He allows us to *choose* whether or not to accept Him. When you conform to God's plan and ask for His help, you remove the barriers. Think about it . . . the greatest power in the universe, the living God, *working in and through you!* Nothing stands in your way.

TODAY'S THOUGHT

Keeping your faith during a time of intense pain often requires fighting a raging battle in your mind. But God *will* help you. Ask Him.

TODAY: ________

FEELINGS CHECK
Today I feel:

ONE THING I'M GRATEFUL FOR TODAY:

BIBLE VERSE

PSALM 91:4–5 (*NLT*)

He will shield you with his wings. He will shelter you with his feathers. His faithful promises are your armor and protection. Do not be afraid . . .

REFLECTIONS

Sometimes during grief, holding on to faith seems too hard, and you feel inadequate to meet the challenge. Remind yourself that God *will* help you if you ask. I love the picture painted by the Bible verse above . . . the image of God protecting and caring for you, safe beneath His wings. When you are discouraged, remember this picture of your loving Father. Look to Him when you cannot meet the adversity on your own.

TODAY: ________

FEELINGS CHECK
Today I feel:

ONE THING I'M GRATEFUL FOR TODAY:

TODAY'S THOUGHT

Find encouragement daily—use affirmations, read books, meditate on God's Word, talk to a friend . . . or something. *Every day!*

BIBLE VERSE

PSALM 31:24 (*MSG*)

Be brave. Be strong. Don't give up. Expect God to get here soon.

REFLECTIONS

All of us need support, especially during disheartening and challenging times. Your *way* of being encouraged is not as important as being sure you do something every day to keep hope alive. Problems look smaller, tasks seem doable, and progress seems achievable when your spirits are high. *Everything* is better when your attitude is positive, so take steps to stay encouraged.

TODAY'S THOUGHT

Try reciting affirmations aloud. The spoken word carries unmistakable power! For instance, affirm these words, "I rely on God's promises," and "I trust God's character." Say, "God loves me," and "I believe God's Word," or "Whatever happens, God will take care of me."

BIBLE VERSE

ROMANS 4:17 (*NIV*)

". . . the God who gives life to the dead and calls things that are not as though they were."

TODAY: ______

FEELINGS CHECK
Today I feel:

ONE THING I'M GRATEFUL FOR TODAY:

REFLECTIONS

The power of the spoken word appears throughout Scripture. God *spoke* creation into existence; Christians confess their faith *aloud*; and blessings *spoken* over people changed their lives. Harness the power of the spoken word and declare your desired thoughts, attitudes, beliefs, hopes, and dreams *as though they already were*. Affirm the positive and watch what happens!

TODAY:

FEELINGS CHECK
Today I feel:

ONE THING I'M GRATEFUL FOR TODAY:

TODAY'S THOUGHT

Sometimes we don't know what to pray, or because of our states of mind, we don't have the *capacity* to pray.

BIBLE VERSE

Romans 8:26–27 (*NLT*)

And the Holy Spirit helps us in our distress. For we don't even know what we should pray for, nor how we should pray. But the Holy Spirit prays for us . . . And the Father who knows all hearts knows what the Spirit is saying, for the Spirit pleads for us believers in harmony with God's own will.

REFLECTIONS

When we don't know what to pray, or our emotional conditions are such that we *can't* pray (even though we may want to), God promises that the Holy Spirit will *pray for us*. What an awe-inspiring promise! At times during grief, as much as I wanted to, I could not pray. All I was able to do was cry; however, God was doing what I could not do for myself. During those times, I *held tight* to His promise.

TODAY'S THOUGHT

Make a list of your greatest blessings. For whom or what in your life are you most thankful to God?

TODAY: ______

FEELINGS CHECK
Today I feel:

ONE THING I'M GRATEFUL FOR TODAY:

BIBLE VERSE

I THESSALONIANS 5:16–18 (*NIV*)

Be joyful always; pray continually; give thanks in all circumstances, for this is God's will for you in Christ Jesus.

REFLECTIONS

When you are suffering, giving thanks may be difficult to do—but God calls us to give thanks *at all times*. He is with us constantly, in every circumstance. He cares about whatever we are facing. Express your gratitude for His love, focus on your blessings instead of your losses, and your attitude will begin to change. Start recognizing His blessings even in the things you take for granted, and your heart will change.

TODAY:

FEELINGS CHECK
Today I feel:

ONE THING I'M GRATEFUL FOR TODAY:

TODAY'S THOUGHT

Never underestimate the value of talking about your loss, journaling, and doing short exercises from the *STUNNED by Grief* book and journal. They *will* help you to heal.

BIBLE VERSE

PROVERBS 11:14 (*MSG*)

Without good direction, people lose their way; the more wise counsel you follow, the better your chances.

REFLECTIONS

Talking, writing, and doing the exercises are healing tools. Each one is a means of getting your thoughts and feelings to move from the *inside* to the *outside*. The tools are a way to help you confront your feelings and resolve them. Healing is a by-product, and healing is your goal. Work through the pain, so you are able to experience the joy again.

TODAY'S THOUGHT

Who (or what) have you lost? How has your loss affected your life? Facing grief head-on, along with the pain, changes, and adjustments, brings healing.

TODAY: ________

FEELINGS CHECK
Today I feel:

____

____

ONE THING I'M GRATEFUL FOR TODAY:

____

____

____

BIBLE VERSE

II CORINTHIANS 4:16 (*MSG*)

So we're not giving up. How could we! Even though on the outside it often looks like things are falling apart on us, on the inside, where God is making new life, not a day goes by without his unfolding grace.

REFLECTIONS

Loss is a reality, pain is undeniable, and both *demand* attention. You cannot ignore pain and expect it to go away. Write about your loss and how it affects your life, both now and in the future. Before you can accept what has happened and move forward, you will re-examine your loss *repeatedly*—in your mind and in your heart. Remember, grief is a *process.*

TODAY:

FEELINGS CHECK
Today I feel:

ONE THING I'M GRATEFUL FOR TODAY:

REFLECTIONS

A fellow traveler compared grief to a disability—saying that you don't get over it, you just learn to live with it. I agree (in part) with his view, since reminders can always trigger responses to your loss; however, reactions become less intense and less frequent over time. As healing occurs, your focus (and energy) shifts from the past and loss to contemplating the future and creating a new life. Eventually, the reminders become tender memories.

TODAY'S THOUGHT

Healing from grief is not the same as healing from an illness. Remnants of grief remain . . . but healing means you have faced the pain of loss, released it, and are now looking toward the future.

BIBLE VERSE

PSALM 147:3 (*NIV*)

He heals the brokenhearted and binds up their wounds.

TODAY'S THOUGHT

Draw a picture of your broken heart. Describe the elements of your picture and what you have lost—and share this exercise with a close friend or family member.

TODAY: ______

FEELINGS CHECK
Today I feel:

ONE THING I'M GRATEFUL FOR TODAY:

BIBLE VERSE

PROVERBS 16:24 (*NLT*)

Kind words are like honey—sweet to the soul and healthy for the body.

REFLECTIONS

I encourage you to do the exercise and share the result with someone close, even if you are unsure about it. Grief-support members who completed the exercise wholeheartedly confirmed its value. Not only was the activity beneficial to the griever, but talking about the drawing with a loved one helped them appreciate their mutual feelings of loss. Healing and bonding took place.

TODAY:

FEELINGS CHECK
Today I feel:

ONE THING I'M GRATEFUL FOR TODAY:

TODAY'S THOUGHT

The time will finally come to release your grief and your loved one; however, release does not happen immediately and completely—it's a *process.*

BIBLE VERSE

ROMANS 14:7 (*NIV*)

For none of us lives to himself alone and none of us dies to himself alone.

REFLECTIONS

Release does *not* mean forgetting. However, release is a turning point in the grief process, and most people remember when they made this significant decision—the decision to *live again!* Making a choice to re-engage fully in life is a major milestone; however, release does not happen immediately and completely. Remember, it is a process.

TODAY'S THOUGHT

Release also means surrendering your new future to God, *whatever* He has in store for you, regardless of your own ideas.

TODAY: ________

FEELINGS CHECK
Today I feel:

ONE THING I'M GRATEFUL FOR TODAY:

BIBLE VERSE

ACTS 21:14 (*GOD'S WORD*)

. . . *"May the Lord's will be done."*

REFLECTIONS

After my husband died, I struggled with God over my situation. I did not want to be alone for the rest of my life, and everything seemed to be at a standstill. I saw no evidence of any change in the future. Even though I had no idea what God had in store for me, I finally accepted God's will for my life—*whatever* He decided. I relaxed and embraced His peace. Release is critical. *God's* way calls for our will to align with His will.

TODAY:

FEELINGS CHECK
Today I feel:

ONE THING I'M GRATEFUL FOR TODAY:

TODAY'S THOUGHT

Don't look back, you're not going that way.
Remind yourself to keep looking forward.
Endings become new beginnings.

BIBLE VERSE

Psalm 62:5–6 (*NLT*)

I wait quietly before God, for my hope is in him. He alone is my rock and my salvation, my fortress where I will not be shaken.

REFLECTIONS

At last, I accepted my unchangeable reality and started letting go of the past. I recognized the truth about my own life because of my loss, and knew that if I were going to build a fulfilling life again, I had to look to the future. At first, looking forward was not automatic; however, as time went on, I became more accustomed to thinking about new beginnings. God wants to be our rock and our salvation. We can *confidently* wait *in Him* as we look forward.

TODAY'S THOUGHT

Describe ways in which you are beginning to release your loved one or your loss.

TODAY: _______

FEELINGS CHECK
Today I feel:

ONE THING I'M GRATEFUL FOR TODAY:

BIBLE VERSE

JOB 11:18 (*GOD'S WORD*)

"You will feel confident because there's hope, and you will look around and rest in safety."

REFLECTIONS

I selected cherished items too valuable to risk losing—and placed them in a book for my daughter. This collection included special family photographs, personal letters and cards, my husband's memorial booklet, and students' letters and drawings describing his impact on their lives. Creating this book was an act of release. I also started doing new things by myself, developing social contacts, getting involved in classes and activities, and making new goals. These were all ways of releasing my loss.

TODAY:

FEELINGS CHECK
Today I feel:

ONE THING I'M GRATEFUL FOR TODAY:

TODAY'S THOUGHT

Remapping is a personal process of pain and sadness, acceptance, release, discovery, and renewal unique to each individual. It's not a canned, predictable, step-by-step checklist—and it requires time and others.

BIBLE VERSE

PROVERBS 13:19 (*MSG*)

Souls who follow their hearts thrive . . .

REFLECTIONS

Pain is personal and no one can fully understand yours, just as another person cannot fully experience your joy. Remapping is a deeply personal experience, even though you cannot successfully accomplish it without support from others. Remapping is a *process*, but it does not operate like clockwork. Back-and-forth movement, a jagged path, and repetition are normal as you work your way through. While the actions are universal, your journey is unique.

TODAY'S THOUGHT

When you lose someone or something, you are left with abrupt dead-ends in place of roads and bridges you had before. Accepting change requires courage and flexibility. It happens little by little. And sometimes you have to develop new ties . . .

QUOTE

It's not so much that we're afraid of change or so in love with the old ways, but it's that place in between that we fear . . . . It's like being between trapezes. It's Linus when his blanket is in the dryer. There's nothing to hold on to.

—Marilyn Ferguson

TODAY: ______

FEELINGS CHECK
Today I feel:

ONE THING I'M GRATEFUL FOR TODAY:

REFLECTIONS

Loss brings change, and part of remapping is adjusting to those changes. Relationships, interests, experiences, plans, dreams, attachments, and ways of thinking connect you to your world and other people. Because of loss, some changes occur abruptly and others happen gradually. Some links completely fall apart and new ones are necessary. Certain connections end and others undergo a transition. Remapping requires change. Keep in mind that change *can be* good.

TODAY:

FEELINGS CHECK
Today I feel:

ONE THING I'M GRATEFUL FOR TODAY:

REFLECTIONS

We *need* to grieve—because grieving is how we let go of what we no longer have. We grieve so we can again embrace the good things in our lives. Grieving is positive. Do not be afraid to grieve or apologetic about your need to grieve. God wired you for grief—and remapping.

TODAY'S THOUGHT

God *designed* grieving to allow us to handle our inevitable losses. Grieving is a process that enables us to let go of someone (or something) we no longer have.

BIBLE VERSE

ROMANS 5:3–5 (*NIV*)

. . . we know that suffering produces perseverance; perseverance, character; and character, hope. And hope does not disappoint us, because God has poured out his love into our hearts by the Holy Spirit, whom he has given us.

TODAY'S THOUGHT

The Bible is clear that we were not made to grieve alone, but in community. So why are we uncomfortable (even ashamed) to share our grief with others or let them know we are grieving?

TODAY: ______

FEELINGS CHECK
Today I feel:

______

______

ONE THING I'M GRATEFUL FOR TODAY:

______

______

______

BIBLE VERSE

PROVERBS 11:2 (*NLT*)

Pride leads to disgrace, but with humility comes wisdom.

REFLECTIONS

God provided a means for us to reconcile loss, and throughout the Bible, we read accounts of people grieving. Even Jesus wept. However, we are often times embarrassed by grief, both in ourselves and in others. Grieving is a natural, necessary process. But don't grieve alone. We need each other.

TODAY: ________

FEELINGS CHECK
Today I feel:

ONE THING I'M GRATEFUL FOR TODAY:

TODAY'S THOUGHT

Remapping is positive and healthy. It represents growth, learning, and change. Don't let the prospect frighten or overwhelm you. Just begin.

BIBLE VERSE

JOB 11:13, 18 (*NLT*)

If only you would prepare your heart and lift up your hands to him in prayer!
You will have courage because you will have hope. You will be protected and will rest in safety.

REFLECTIONS

While everyone does not readily embrace change, remapping is *not* negative. Instead, it is positive and healthy. Keep the goal in mind—going full circle through grief—so you can release the pain and wholly open yourself up to new life. *Start somewhere* by doing *something,* and you will see things fall into place. Once progress begins, your anxiety will lessen.

TODAY'S THOUGHT

Expect to go through setbacks, but that is okay. Setbacks are normal. Just keep going down the path.

TODAY: ______

FEELINGS CHECK
Today I feel:

ONE THING I'M GRATEFUL FOR TODAY:

BIBLE VERSE

HEBREWS 12:7, 11 (*NIV*)

Endure hardship as discipline . . .

No discipline seems pleasant at the time, but painful. Later on, however, it produces a harvest of righteousness and peace for those who have been trained by it.

REFLECTIONS

Remapping does not follow a direct path down a predetermined road on a given timetable. You *will* undoubtedly experience setbacks, but knowing what to expect will prepare you before obstacles occur—so they will not overwhelm you. Just recognize the path is jagged and *keep going.* And remember to be kind to yourself when you stumble. You *will* be okay in time.

TODAY: ______

FEELINGS CHECK
Today I feel:

ONE THING I'M GRATEFUL FOR TODAY:

TODAY'S THOUGHT

Don't look too far ahead—and don't forget to ask God for help.

BIBLE VERSE

PROVERBS 23:18 (*NIV*)

There is surely a future hope for you, and your hope will not be cut off.

REFLECTIONS

Don't take on too much—and don't think about how far you still have to go. Just think about *today* and what you must do *right now*. At first, you'll be living from minute to minute . . . then hour to hour . . . and finally the timetable begins to stretch out. Grief is a process taken in *steps*. Allow the process to unfold naturally, gradually—and cooperate with it. You will be more peaceful when you approach grief this way.

TODAY'S THOUGHT

Don't be too hard
on yourself.

TODAY: ______

FEELINGS CHECK
Today I feel:

ONE THING I'M GRATEFUL FOR TODAY:

BIBLE VERSE

ECCLESIASTES 7:8–9 (*NLT*)

Finishing is better than starting. Patience is better than pride. Don't be quick-tempered, for anger is the friend of fools.

REFLECTIONS

By understanding grief, you will be prepared when things don't go as expected. Grief is one of the single toughest experiences in life—and one we are least prepared to face. Be gentle with yourself. I expect you are doing the best you can, so remind yourself of that. Just keep going down the path.

TODAY: ________

FEELINGS CHECK
Today I feel:

ONE THING I'M GRATEFUL FOR TODAY:

TODAY'S THOUGHT

Trust others who have traveled before you.

BIBLE VERSE

PROVERBS 4:7 (*NLT*)

Getting wisdom is the most important thing you can do! And whatever else you do, get good judgment.

REFLECTIONS

When my husband died, I knew nothing about grief. I did not know what to do, where I was going, or whether I could find my way through the confusion. I read books by people who had already traveled the road. They had made it through grief, and I trusted that if they had done it, so could I. Before I could rely on my ability, I trusted their words, experiences, and reassurances. I kept looking to God for help. I hope you will do the same.

TODAY'S THOUGHT

You cannot live a healthy, happy life if
you are unable to fully grieve your losses.
The alternative is tragic.

TODAY: ______

FEELINGS CHECK
Today I feel:

ONE THING I'M GRATEFUL FOR TODAY:

QUOTE

Anything in life that we don't accept will simply make trouble for us until we make peace with it.

—Shakti Gawain

REFLECTIONS

Failing to grieve your losses fully will prevent you from leading a healthy, happy life in the future. No one wants to feel the pain—but remember, the pain will not last forever *if* you face it and work through it. Make up your mind to do whatever is necessary to get well. Come to terms with your loss, so you can move forward.

TODAY:

FEELINGS CHECK
Today I feel:

ONE THING I'M GRATEFUL FOR TODAY:

TODAY'S THOUGHT

Remapping is more valuable than gold, so precious you cannot put a price on it. We are talking about your life. *Your life.*

BIBLE VERSE

Ephesians 2:10 (*NLT*)

For we are God's masterpiece. He has created us anew in Christ Jesus, so that we can do the good things he planned for us long ago.

REFLECTIONS

Hope . . . tomorrow . . . life. What does your picture look like? The value of remapping is immeasurable—because it affects the quality of your future. Can you put a price on it? I would *never* have chosen to lose my husband, but it happened. However, I will not sacrifice the rest of my life because he died. I chose to make the best of what I still have. You, too, can make the same choice. Trust God's plans for your future.

TODAY'S THOUGHT

One of the greatest stumbling-blocks, especially among widows and widowers, is having no idea how to rebuild their lives without their mates. Keep an open mind and experiment.

TODAY: ______

FEELINGS CHECK
Today I feel:

ONE THING I'M GRATEFUL FOR TODAY:

QUOTE

We cannot become what we need to be by remaining what we are.

—Max DePree

REFLECTIONS

When you're suddenly alone after losing a mate, the changes seem insurmountable. At first, survival is the goal. However, when you finally want to rebuild your life, you probably do not have a clue how to begin. Shake off self-conscious and hypersensitive feelings, and then cultivate a sense of adventure—even if you have to dig deep to find it. Try *something,* and if that does not work, try *something else.* Start somewhere. Each step gets easier.

TODAY: ______

FEELINGS CHECK
Today I feel:

ONE THING I'M GRATEFUL FOR TODAY:

TODAY'S THOUGHT

Don't take yourself too seriously, and be willing to experiment and fail. Step out and try something new, even if the change is small.

QUOTE

We experiment and copy and ultimately find our own way to put paint on the canvas.

—Kim Fancher Lordier

REFLECTIONS

Experiment. Try something new. Start out with little changes until you're more at ease testing the untested waters. Begin with personal changes close to home and expand when you are ready. Start out small, but *start*. You are more capable (and more brave) than you think. Be patient!

TODAY'S THOUGHT

You *are* able to do many things alone. You may not have considered that idea before, but try it. Conquering this fear (or stigma) is liberating!

TODAY: ______

FEELINGS CHECK
Today I feel:

ONE THING I'M GRATEFUL FOR TODAY:

BIBLE VERSE

JOSHUA 1:9 (*MSG*)

. . . *"Strength! Courage! Don't be timid; don't get discouraged. God, your God, is with you every step you take."*

REFLECTIONS

You may not be used to doing things alone, but you *can* overcome your initial reserve and just do it. Defeating this fear gives you a feeling of power, control, and freedom. Restrictions fade and your options multiply. You'll be free to make a 'spur of the moment' decision to do something . . . and do it! You won't have to wait for anyone else. *Experiment* with courage.

TODAY:

FEELINGS CHECK
Today I feel:

ONE THING I'M GRATEFUL FOR TODAY:

REFLECTIONS

Remapping involves change, and change is uncomfortable. Change involves risk-taking—but success builds each time you test new things—and *risking* gets easier. Adjustments are part of the moving-forward process. Look for ways to fulfill the longings of your heart as you embrace change. God will help you.

TODAY'S THOUGHT

Look for opportunities to invite new people (and activities) into your life. Be more approachable and available.

BIBLE VERSE

ROMANS 12:9–10, 16 (*MSG*)

Love from the center of who you are; don't fake it . . . Be good friends who love deeply; practice playing second fiddle.

Get along with each other; don't be stuck-up. Make friends with nobodies; don't be the great somebody.

TODAY'S THOUGHT

Eliminate 'impossible' from your vocabulary.
Program your thinking with powerful words:
"I can," "I will," and "I do."

TODAY:

FEELINGS CHECK
Today I feel:

ONE THING I'M GRATEFUL FOR TODAY:

BIBLE VERSE

MATTHEW 17:20 (*MSG*)

"Because you're not yet taking God *seriously," said Jesus. "The simple truth is that if you had a mere kernel of faith, a poppy seed, say, you would tell this mountain, 'Move!' and it would move. There is nothing you wouldn't be able to tackle."*

REFLECTIONS

What we do (or don't do) depends on our attitudes. What have you decided? Are you going to let obstacles stop you? No! *Set your mind* and refuse to give up. Reprogram your thinking with powerful words. You may be surprised to realize all you *can* do. Discover some great new things about yourself.

TODAY:

FEELINGS CHECK
Today I feel:

ONE THING I'M GRATEFUL FOR TODAY:

REFLECTIONS

Approach your situation with an open mind and creativity. Begin to accept (and appreciate) the benefits of solitude as a way to know yourself and God in ways you may not have recognized before. Cultivate serenity. Gather your courage and move toward the future, even if you see only a sliver of light right now. Get past the negatives and see the *possibilities!*

TODAY'S THOUGHT

Look at your new freedom as a positive prospect instead of a perpetual prison. Be courageous enough to step out into the light.

BIBLE VERSE

II Samuel 22:29 (*MSG*)

Suddenly, God, your light floods my path, God drives out the darkness.

TODAY'S THOUGHT

Remapping involves trial and error. When you have victories, even small ones, you will gain momentum that can transform your life and put you on track.

TODAY: ______

FEELINGS CHECK
Today I feel:

ONE THING I'M GRATEFUL FOR TODAY:

BIBLE VERSE

II Chronicles 32:7–8 (*MSG*)

. . . "Be strong! Take courage! Don't be intimidated . . . we have our God to help us and fight for us!"

REFLECTIONS

When you decide not to give up—and keep taking small steps—victories start happening. Small triumphs produce momentum, transforming your thinking and your life. Once you plant your feet on the right track, the wonder and joy of life will again be yours. Strength will grow inside of you, reminding you how far you have traveled and how much you have grown. You are on the road to healing.

TODAY:

FEELINGS CHECK
Today I feel:

ONE THING I'M GRATEFUL FOR TODAY:

TODAY'S THOUGHT

Your life will never be the same, but how you allow grief to affect you is *your choice*. Grief *can be* a positively defining, life-changing experience.

BIBLE VERSE

II Corinthians 9:8 (*MSG*)

God can pour on the blessings in astonishing ways so that you're ready for anything and everything, more than just ready to do what needs to be done.

REFLECTIONS

No one would willingly choose the pain of loss; however, much of what happens to us in life is not up to us. Still, we decide how we respond to every experience, and our choices determine our lives. My encounter with loss was a defining experience. Life, viewed through the lens of loss, takes on a new dimension. The same can be true for you. The decision is yours.

TODAY'S THOUGHT

Loss can teach us valuable life lessons. When someone (or something) we love most is torn from us, we discover who we *really* are and what is *truly* important. Life suddenly looks different.

BIBLE VERSE

PSALM 119:59 (*MSG*)

When I took a long, careful look at your ways, I got my feet back on the trail you blazed.

TODAY: ______

FEELINGS CHECK
Today I feel:

ONE THING I'M GRATEFUL FOR TODAY:

REFLECTIONS

Loss exposes life in a basic way. Pretenses disappear and an overwhelming sense of what matters becomes key. *Significance* comes into sharp focus. Life has changed forever, because you can never forget such important lessons learned. Grief changes your perspective.

TODAY:

FEELINGS CHECK
Today I feel:

ONE THING I'M GRATEFUL FOR TODAY:

REFLECTIONS

Think about what really matters to you now. Consider all you have learned, and decide how you are going to use your insight. Lessons gained through loss did not emerge easily. I challenge you to use your wisdom constructively, and make your life (and the lives of those you love) richer because of your painful journey. Step out, risk, and live mindfully.

TODAY'S THOUGHT

The question becomes, "What is truly significant to you, and what will you do with all you've learned?" Will you take the risk and experience life in a new way—an unfamiliar way?

BIBLE VERSE

PHILIPPIANS 3:12–14 (*NLT*)

. . . I keep working toward that day when I will finally be all that Christ Jesus saved me for and wants me to be . . . I am focusing all my energies on this one thing: Forgetting the past and looking forward to what lies ahead, I strain to reach the end of the race and receive the prize . . .

TODAY'S THOUGHT

What steps are you
taking to remap your life?

TODAY: ______

FEELINGS CHECK
Today I feel:

ONE THING
I'M GRATEFUL
FOR TODAY:

BIBLE VERSE

JAMES 1:4–6 (*NIV*)

Perseverance must finish its work so that you may be mature and complete, not lacking anything. If any of you lacks wisdom, he should ask God, who gives generously to all without finding fault, and it will be given to him. But when he asks, he must believe and not doubt . . .

REFLECTIONS

Are you moving forward? If you feel trapped, what do you need to do? What is holding you back? Do not allow others to pressure you to move ahead too fast, but slowly keep taking steps to remap your life. If you need help, ask for it. Do whatever is necessary to find healing and start living again. *Life* is worth *living.*

TODAY: ______

FEELINGS CHECK
Today I feel:

ONE THING I'M GRATEFUL FOR TODAY:

TODAY'S THOUGHT

After a loss, laughter seems impossible for a while; however, grievers desperately need to find relief from their all-encompassing pain.

BIBLE VERSE

PROVERBS 15:13 (*MSG*)

A cheerful heart brings a smile to your face; a sad heart makes it hard to get through the day.

REFLECTIONS

Profound sadness accompanies loss, and minimizing or dismissing genuine feelings is not healthy. While laughter will be uncomfortable right away, grievers seriously need relief (even briefly) from their intense pain. Laughter offers a healthy release. Continual sadness brings exhaustion, so rely on laughter as a "healing" escape.

TODAY'S THOUGHT

Grievers sometimes allow laughter and humor to make them feel guilty or disloyal. Release that kind of thinking. Laughter is not only okay, it will boost healing.

TODAY: ______

FEELINGS CHECK
Today I feel:

ONE THING I'M GRATEFUL FOR TODAY:

BIBLE VERSE

PROVERBS 14:30 (*NLT*)

A relaxed attitude lengthens life . . .

REFLECTIONS

Feeling guilty and disloyal when you laugh is a common early response to grief, but quickly set those feelings free. You *need* to laugh! Laughter is a miracle drug, and it produces an amazing range of positive effects—mentally, physically, emotionally, socially, and spiritually. Researchers have widely examined and verified the healing effects of laughter. Allow laughter to do its *miraculous work* in you.

TODAY:

FEELINGS CHECK
Today I feel:

ONE THING I'M GRATEFUL FOR TODAY:

TODAY'S THOUGHT

Intense laughter, even if it's *faked*, produces the same effects as real laughter. So what are you waiting for? You will not only feel better, but your body will be healthier.

BIBLE VERSE

PROVERBS 17:22 (*MSG*)

A cheerful disposition is good for your health; gloom and doom leave you bone-tired.

REFLECTIONS

Researchers have proven that even faked intense laughter produces positive effects in the body. Laughter stimulates healing; yields aerobic benefits; increases energy; lowers stress; connects you with others; enhances learning . . . and on and on. What are you waiting for? Make laughter a priority in your life.

TODAY'S THOUGHT

Scientific evidence confirms that emotions, moods, thoughts, and attitudes have biological effects. There *is* a biology of hope!

TODAY: ______

FEELINGS CHECK
Today I feel:

______

______

ONE THING I'M GRATEFUL FOR TODAY:

______

______

______

BIBLE VERSE

PROVERBS 15:30 (*MSG*)

A twinkle in the eye means joy in the heart, and good news makes you feel fit as a fiddle.

REFLECTIONS

Research confirms the biological effects of laughter on the human body, and its effects are not only real but also powerful. Dr. Norman Cousins' research concluded that hope positively influences the immune system and, conversely, depression produces a negative result. He effectively used *laughter therapy* on himself and his patients in an intensive effort to fight grave illnesses. Laughter is powerful medicine. Try it—and see for yourself!

TODAY: ______

FEELINGS CHECK
Today I feel:

ONE THING I'M GRATEFUL FOR TODAY:

TODAY'S THOUGHT

When your attitude reveals a strong sense of humor, positive effects spread to all parts of your life. Don't worry if you're in short supply—a sense of humor can be *developed!*

BIBLE VERSE

PROVERBS 15:15 (*MSG*)

A miserable heart means a miserable life; a cheerful heart fills the day with song.

REFLECTIONS

Notice the evidence researchers have uncovered. Positive effects of laughter and a sense of humor spread into all areas of your life. Science links a well-developed sense of humor to happiness, health, success, greater creativity, better coping skills and intellectual performance, and more. Positivity affects your attitude, your perception, and *everything else!* You can *grow* your sense of humor. Try it and see what happens.

TODAY'S THOUGHT

Act your way into a feeling until the feeling becomes real. By doing this, you convert a negative to a positive. Do not deny your emotions, but sometimes you need *relief* from grief.

TODAY: ______

FEELINGS CHECK
Today I feel:

ONE THING I'M GRATEFUL FOR TODAY:

QUOTE

A good laugh and a long sleep are the best cures in the doctor's book.

—Irish Proverb

REFLECTIONS

Grief can be draining and seem hopeless at times, so it's easy to fall prey to negative attitudes, moods, and thoughts. Making a conscious effort to act contrary to those feelings—until the feelings change—brings relief. Instead of giving in to negative emotions or thoughts, *change* them. Grief work remains, but rest is essential, too. Look for things that make you laugh.

TODAY:

FEELINGS CHECK
Today I feel:

ONE THING I'M GRATEFUL FOR TODAY:

REFLECTIONS

Laughter, and temporary relief from pain, will keep hope alive as you work through grief. Hope is *critical.* Hope is the life force that keeps you going when you think you cannot go on. *Believe* you have a future. Think about what is good in your life, and set your mind on anything positive. *Fight* for hope, and ask God to help you.

TODAY'S THOUGHT

Relief from pain helps keep hope alive,
and hope is as essential to life as air and water.
Do whatever is necessary to fuel your hope.

BIBLE VERSE

II CORINTHIANS 4:18 (*NLT*)

So we don't look at the troubles we can see right now; rather, we look forward to what we have not yet seen. For the troubles we see will soon be over, but the joys to come will last forever.

TODAY'S THOUGHT

You have a life after grief—and it's worth the effort to get there. Even if you are not convinced, trust me (and others) who have already confirmed this truth in our lives.

TODAY: ______

FEELINGS CHECK
Today I feel:

ONE THING I'M GRATEFUL FOR TODAY:

BIBLE VERSE

I JOHN 5:13–15 (*MSG*)

My purpose in writing is simply this: that you who believe in God's Son will know beyond the shadow of a doubt that you have eternal life, the reality and not the illusion. And how bold and free we then become in his presence, freely asking according to his will, sure that he's listening . . .

REFLECTIONS

Laughter . . . hope . . . courage . . . perseverance . . . life. You *have* a future beyond grief—and persistence is worth the price to find out what God has for you. Others have discovered the truth: you *will* make it through, and life *will be* good once more. I wondered whether I would laugh or be happy again. Such feelings are natural, but trust others who are farther down the path. You *can* make it through. You *do* have a future. And your future *can be* bright.

TODAY: ______

FEELINGS CHECK
Today I feel:

ONE THING I'M GRATEFUL FOR TODAY:

TODAY'S THOUGHT

What are you doing to bring laughter into your life? Laughter is important—so *make* it a priority! Think about what you can do.

QUOTE

We don't laugh because we're happy—we're happy because we laugh.

—William James

REFLECTIONS

Laughter carries benefits you may only be able to glimpse right now, but if for no other immediate reason, laugh because it will make you feel better! What will you do to stimulate laughter in your life? Make it a priority *now.* If you can't think of a reason to laugh—then fake it. You will still realize its benefits.

TODAY'S THOUGHT

Unless you want to be continually frustrated and discouraged, set aside your timing and focus on accepting God's timing. The two will almost certainly be different.

TODAY: ______

FEELINGS CHECK
Today I feel:

ONE THING I'M GRATEFUL FOR TODAY:

BIBLE VERSE

II PETER 3:8–9 (*GOD'S WORD*)

Dear friends, don't ignore this fact: One day with the Lord is like a thousand years, and a thousand years are like one day. The Lord isn't slow to do what he promised, as some people think. Rather, he is patient for your sake . . .

REFLECTIONS

Not only does God think differently than we do, but He works outside of time constraints. He sees past, present, and future—so He sees our situations with insight we do not have. Our timing and God's rarely coincide, so we will be less frustrated if we focus on accepting His will instead of being discouraged when things do not happen by our schedules. Trust God's perfectly tailored plan. He loves you and knows what is best *for you.*

TODAY:

FEELINGS CHECK
Today I feel:

ONE THING I'M GRATEFUL FOR TODAY:

TODAY'S THOUGHT

The less you focus on *time* and the more you focus on *living*, the less frustrated you will be.

BIBLE VERSE

PSALM 90:12 (*NLT*)

Teach us to make the most of our time, so that we may grow in wisdom.

REFLECTIONS

Working your way through grief and starting to re-engage in life are more than enough to occupy your mind. Concentrate on *living* instead of timing, and make the most of the present. Discover what you can from your grief experience, and life will be more rewarding.

TODAY'S THOUGHT

Learning to rest in God does not come naturally. However, God does not want anxiety and turmoil to consume our lives. He wants us to be at peace and trust Him.

BIBLE VERSE

PSALM 119:114 (*MSG*)

You're my place of quiet retreat; I wait for your Word to renew me.

TODAY: ______

FEELINGS CHECK
Today I feel:

ONE THING I'M GRATEFUL FOR TODAY:

REFLECTIONS

Human beings are headstrong, and we are predisposed to retain control. We *think* we know what is best, so resting in God does not come naturally. But God wants us to be at peace and trust Him fully. He does not want us to live anxious, turmoil-ridden lives—questioning every twist and turn, constantly worrying. Can you *trust* Him to work out His plans for you? *Will* you trust him?

TODAY:

FEELINGS CHECK
Today I feel:

ONE THING I'M GRATEFUL FOR TODAY:

REFLECTIONS

When we become distracted from God and grow anxious, the enemy (Satan) achieves his goal. God promises to take care of all our needs, and He wants us to trust Him for *everything*. He knows all about us, down to the number of hairs on our heads. Worry is useless, unproductive, and even destructive—so seek God, trust Him to take care of you, and thank Him when He does. Your trust will not be in vain.

TODAY'S THOUGHT

Worry indicates a lack of faith. The Bible teaches us to trust God for everything. Will you?

BIBLE VERSE

MATTHEW 6:34 (*MSG*)

"Give your entire attention to what God is doing right now, and don't get worked up about what may or may not happen tomorrow. God will help you deal with whatever hard things come up when the time comes."

TODAY'S THOUGHT

By keeping control of our lives in our hands, we miss God's best for us. His plans, and His thoughts, are *far beyond* anything we can visualize!

TODAY: ______

FEELINGS CHECK
Today I feel:

ONE THING I'M GRATEFUL FOR TODAY:

BIBLE VERSE

I CORINTHIANS 2:9 (*NLT*)

. . . *"No eye has seen, no ear has heard, and no mind has imagined what God has prepared for those who love him."*

REFLECTIONS

God's plans outshine *anything* we can conceive on our own. By attempting to maintain control ourselves, we miss the amazement of God's perfect, tailor-made plan for us. Do you *think about* what God has planned for you? Aren't you *curious*?

TODAY:

FEELINGS CHECK
Today I feel:

ONE THING I'M GRATEFUL FOR TODAY:

TODAY'S THOUGHT

Satan, the great deceiver, will try *anything* to agitate us, worry us, and shake our trust in God. Recognize the signals—and stop him! Do not let Satan gain the upper hand.

BIBLE VERSE

JAMES 4:7 (*AMP*)

So be subject to God. Resist the devil [stand firm against him], and he will flee from you.

REFLECTIONS

God constantly stretches us to help us grow, and how we handle life's hard times influences the blessings and responsibilities He gives us. In addition, deceitful forces work to sidetrack us, so watch for Satan's warning signs. When anxiety overpowers you—pause, recognize the source, and put a stop to it. Fear is not from God! Neither are accusation nor condemnation. Stay faithful and God will *never* let you down.

TODAY'S THOUGHT

You do not have to *do* everything yourself—you just have to be *willing* to be changed by God and submit to His changes. God can use *everything*, even tragedy, to achieve good.

TODAY: ______

FEELINGS CHECK
Today I feel:

ONE THING I'M GRATEFUL FOR TODAY:

BIBLE VERSE

ROMANS 8:28 (*NLT*)

And we know that God causes everything to work together for the good of those who love God and are called according to his purpose for them.

ROMANS 12:2 (*NLT*)

Don't copy the behavior and customs of this world, but let God transform you into a new person by changing the way you think . . .

REFLECTIONS

When you become a Christian, God promises to *supernaturally* transform you from the inside out. You cannot do everything yourself, but you can yield to God. Submission to His changes is all He asks. And God is able to cause everything, even pain and tragedy, to work together for your good when you follow Him. He promises! I want that promise fulfilled in my life. How about you?

TODAY:

FEELINGS CHECK
Today I feel:

ONE THING I'M GRATEFUL FOR TODAY:

REFLECTIONS

Faith *activates* God's power in your life! Without faith, the Bible teaches that it is impossible to please God. Even a small amount of faith is sufficient. *Expect* God to turn things around for you. Remember, He is able to change anything and everything, completely and instantly. Believe God for great things and open the pipeline of faith.

TODAY'S THOUGHT

God meets us at the level of our expectations—so we get *to choose* how much He blesses us. Remember, a single act by God can change everything *completely*, *dramatically*, and *instantly*.

BIBLE VERSE

MATTHEW 9:29 (*NIV*)

. . . "According to your faith will it be done to you" . . .

TODAY'S THOUGHT

What areas of your life do you need to release to God's timing? *Can* you release them? If not, talk to God about whatever is holding you back.

TODAY: ______

FEELINGS CHECK
Today I feel:

ONE THING I'M GRATEFUL FOR TODAY:

BIBLE VERSE

PSALM 55:22 (*MSG*)

Pile your troubles on God's shoulders—he'll carry your load, he'll help you out. He'll never let good people topple into ruin.

REFLECTIONS

Don't give up—keep waiting on God. Remember that His timing and yours will rarely be the same. However, God is in complete control, and He *loves* you. Trust Him to do what is best, at just the right time. If you are wrestling with God's timing, talk to Him about it. Tell Him you're trying, but you need His help.

TODAY: ______

FEELINGS CHECK
Today I feel:

ONE THING I'M GRATEFUL FOR TODAY:

TODAY'S THOUGHT

Sometimes, we gradually become so wrapped up in the preferences and needs of another person that we lose part of our identity. Look deep within—and honestly get to know yourself again.

BIBLE VERSE

PSALM 4:4 (*NIV*)

. . . search your hearts and be silent.

REFLECTIONS

Change requires adjustments, both internal and external. During remapping, "renewal" is a suitable time to step back and look objectively at yourself and your situation. Be honest as you evaluate where you are and where you want to go. Search yourself. Face the truth as you uncover it, and rediscover who you really are.

TODAY'S THOUGHT

"*I never took the time to be me . . . I have always been someone for somebody,*" a widow wrote. Who are you and what do you want? What kind of changes would you like to make?

BIBLE VERSE

PROVERBS 15:14 (*NLT*)

A wise person is hungry for truth . . .

TODAY: ______

FEELINGS CHECK
Today I feel:

ONE THING I'M GRATEFUL FOR TODAY:

REFLECTIONS

Evaluate how you need to grow and change. Think about what you would like to learn. Look at your strengths and weaknesses, and figure out what you truly like. Rediscover yourself! Take risks and make necessary changes.

TODAY: ______

FEELINGS CHECK
Today I feel:

ONE THING
I'M GRATEFUL
FOR TODAY:

REFLECTIONS

In our world, solitude is difficult to enter. We are accustomed to constant interaction and distraction, whether in person or by phone, internet, or TV. However, certain pursuits *require* peace and quiet. You cannot connect with God while bombarded by noise and confusion. His *still small voice* cannot be heard above the clamor of competing influences. Solitude is a place where you discover treasures you cannot find anywhere else. So get alone, be quiet, and *listen*.

TODAY'S THOUGHT

Solitude means being alone, but it does not mean being lonely. Solitude gives you time to think, remember, create, be alone with God, and listen for His voice. Cultivate this *precious* ground!

BIBLE VERSE

LUKE 5:16 (*NIV*)

But Jesus often withdrew to lonely places and prayed.

TODAY'S THOUGHT

Are you comfortable with quiet and solitude? If so, write about its blessings. If not, why is solitude distressing, and what can you do to capture its blessings?

BIBLE VERSE

ISAIAH 30:15 (*NIV*)

. . . in quietness and trust is your strength . . .

TODAY: ______

FEELINGS CHECK
Today I feel:

ONE THING I'M GRATEFUL FOR TODAY:

REFLECTIONS

'Noise' constantly bombards us, vying for attention. Since noise is the norm, silence can be uneasy. For a time, I could hardly stand to be at home without something turned on to drown the silence—*anything* to quench my feeling of being alone. I realized I had made major strides when I could be alone (and quiet) in my home and feel serene. Busyness steals your attention from activities that bring healing. Do not avoid solitude.

TODAY: ______

FEELINGS CHECK
Today I feel:

ONE THING
I'M GRATEFUL
FOR TODAY:

REFLECTIONS

You may have developed a closer relationship with God because of challenges faced during grief. Perhaps you have discovered untapped reserves of strength and determination you did not realize you have. Maybe you have formed new, fulfilling relationships or changed the way you view life. Positive outcomes *are* possible from grief. What have you discovered?

TODAY'S THOUGHT

Has your grief brought about any positive results? If not, can you *imagine* something positive as an outcome of your painful experience?

BIBLE VERSE

EPHESIANS 3:16–17 (*NLT*)

I pray that from his glorious, unlimited resources he will give you mighty inner strength through his Holy Spirit. And I pray that Christ will be more and more at home in your hearts as you trust in him. May your roots go down deep into the soil of God's marvelous love.

TODAY'S THOUGHT

Where are you in the remapping process? (See diagram in the Appendix.) Discuss actions you still need to take. Is anything holding you back?

TODAY:

FEELINGS CHECK
Today I feel:

ONE THING I'M GRATEFUL FOR TODAY:

BIBLE VERSE

PROVERBS 4:25–27 (*NLT*)

Look straight ahead, and fix your eyes on what lies before you. Mark out a straight path for your feet; then stick to the path and stay safe. Don't get sidetracked . . .

REFLECTIONS

What is your position on the 'remapping' path? Have you traveled halfway or farther? Have your thoughts become less self-centered? Have your priorities changed? Are you thinking about the future more often than the past? Is anything preventing you from moving completely through the process, and if so, how can you overcome that obstacle?

TODAY: ________

FEELINGS CHECK
Today I feel:

ONE THING I'M GRATEFUL FOR TODAY:

TODAY'S THOUGHT

Name one blessing
that came from your pain.

BIBLE VERSE

PSALM 56:3 (*NIV*)

When I am afraid, I will trust in you.

REFLECTIONS

Do you trust God more now than before? Do you view life through a different lens? How have your priorities changed? Do you want to modify your lifestyle? Are relationships more important to you now? Do you want to help other people? How have *you* changed?

TODAY'S THOUGHT

Where is your hope anchored? Is it in yourself and your own strength, in someone else, or in material possessions? Is your hope in God? What can you *dependably* count on?

TODAY: ______

FEELINGS CHECK
Today I feel:

______

______

ONE THING I'M GRATEFUL FOR TODAY:

______

______

______

BIBLE VERSE

Psalm 25:3 (*NIV*)

No one whose hope is in you will ever be put to shame . . .

Isaiah 40:31 (*NIV*)

. . . but those who hope in the Lord will renew their strength. They will soar on wings like eagles; they will run and not grow weary, they will walk and not be faint.

REFLECTIONS

What is the source of your hope? Is your hope secure in God? Or is your hope fastened to an unstable foundation? Think about where you have placed your trust. The *source* is key.

TODAY:

FEELINGS CHECK
Today I feel:

ONE THING I'M GRATEFUL FOR TODAY:

TODAY'S THOUGHT

What is the biggest, most unbelievable desire you have for your life? Now consider this: God has bigger (and better) plans *specifically created for you*!

BIBLE VERSE

EPHESIANS 3:20 (*NLT*)

. . . By his mighty power at work within us, he is able to accomplish infinitely more than we would ever dare to ask or hope.

REFLECTIONS

God's plan for our lives is a great adventure! What will you do with what God has allowed you to face? Will you embrace God's unique plan for you? Try relinquishing control and see where the path leads. No doubt, you will be amazed. God can do more than you could *ever* dream!

TODAY'S THOUGHT

What purpose(s) have you uncovered because of your pain? How will you live your life differently now?

BIBLE VERSE

II Timothy 2:7 (*MSG*)

Think it over. God will make it all plain.

TODAY: ______

FEELINGS CHECK
Today I feel:

ONE THING I'M GRATEFUL FOR TODAY:

REFLECTIONS

Did tragic loss change the way you live? Have you found a new purpose? Writing is a purpose that evolved from my pain. Because I was wholly unprepared for the repercussions of my husband's death, I want to help others through the fear and uncertainty of grief. Because I have already been there, I want to make your way less frightening and troublesome. What have you discovered?

TODAY:

FEELINGS CHECK
Today I feel:

ONE THING I'M GRATEFUL FOR TODAY:

TODAY'S THOUGHT

Who (or what) surprised or disappointed you the most?

BIBLE VERSE

DEUTERONOMY 31:8 (*NLT*)

"Do not be afraid or discouraged, for the Lord is the one who goes before you. He will be with you; he will neither fail you nor forsake you."

REFLECTIONS

One of the most unexpected and disappointing lessons I learned was that relationships, even long-standing ones, can be adversely affected by death and loss. Unquestionably, death changes things—and I am convinced that people do not understand grief because they struggle over *what to do*. I did not expect to feel isolated or like a stranger to myself, nor did I anticipate my self-confidence wavering.

TODAY'S THOUGHT

How will you know when you are getting better?

TODAY: ______

FEELINGS CHECK
Today I feel:

ONE THING I'M GRATEFUL FOR TODAY:

BIBLE VERSE

PSALM 147:5–6 (*MSG*)

Our Lord is great, with limitless strength; we'll never comprehend what he knows and does. God puts the fallen on their feet again . . .

REFLECTIONS

I knew I was getting better when I realized I had not thought about my husband for almost a full day; I could drive somewhere without crying; I made it through a church service without tears; I started thinking about the future again; I could laugh; I was comfortable being alone in my home; and I no longer dreaded holidays.

TODAY:

FEELINGS CHECK
Today I feel:

ONE THING I'M GRATEFUL FOR TODAY:

REFLECTIONS

Loss has a way of putting life in perspective. Picture the way a magnifying glass allows you to see things you cannot see without it, and how this tool brings everything into sharp, vivid focus. A griever grows impatient with trivial, meaningless matters. Significant things become *clearly* crucial. And inconsequential things fall aside.

TODAY'S THOUGHT

How have your priorities changed since your loss?

BIBLE VERSE

MATTHEW 6:25, 31–32 (*NLT*)

"So I tell you, don't worry about everyday life—whether you have enough food, drink, and clothes. Doesn't life consist of more than food and clothing?"

"So don't worry . . . Your heavenly Father already knows all your needs". . .

TODAY'S THOUGHT

Self-revelations: What new strengths have you discovered in yourself as you have faced your loss?

TODAY: ______

FEELINGS CHECK
Today I feel:

ONE THING I'M GRATEFUL FOR TODAY:

BIBLE VERSE

PHILIPPIANS 4:13 (*NLT*)

For I can do everything with the help of Christ who gives me the strength I need.

REFLECTIONS

Through grief, I discovered reservoirs of strength I did not know I had, and with God's help, I was able to carry on when I thought I could not take another step. My faith grew, and God showed up in unexpected (but sorely needed) ways. I discovered I am more determined than I thought, and I found out that *nothing* in my life is more important than faith in God. What have you learned about yourself?

TODAY:

FEELINGS CHECK
Today I feel:

ONE THING I'M GRATEFUL FOR TODAY:

TODAY'S THOUGHT

What new realities has death forced you to see?

BIBLE VERSE

HEBREWS 11:1 (*MSG*)

The fundamental fact of existence is that this trust in God, this faith, is the firm foundation under everything that makes life worth living. It's our handle on what we can't see.

REFLECTIONS

Death highlights the fragility of life as nothing else can. *Saying* that life can end any time and *grasping* the fact are not the same. Reality hit me hard. Avoid snags by keeping documents current, e.g., wills, trusts, insurance policies, beneficiaries, deeds, titles, and such. Everyone needs close relationships *already in place,* so they have a support system when a tragedy strikes. When someone dies or a major loss occurs, it is *too late* to prepare.

TODAY'S THOUGHT

I cannot help but laugh every
time I think about . . .

BIBLE VERSE

Romans 12:12 (*NIV*)

Be joyful in hope, patient in affliction, faithful in prayer.

TODAY: ________

FEELINGS CHECK
Today I feel:

ONE THING I'M GRATEFUL FOR TODAY:

REFLECTIONS

I cannot help but smile every time I think about my husband. He had a great sense of humor and an infectious laugh. His laugh was actually more of a *giggle,* and was a stark contrast to his muscular, football-player build. As healing from grief took place, I could think about him and remember such things with tender joy instead of painful tears. Memories of him will stay with me and forever make me smile.

TODAY:

FEELINGS CHECK
Today I feel:

ONE THING I'M GRATEFUL FOR TODAY:

REFLECTIONS

I look forward to traveling places I have never been; acting more spontaneously; reading lots of books; spending time with friends and family; growing deeper in my relationship with God; helping people navigate grief and discover something good through the process; and encouraging others. What do you long to do?

TODAY'S THOUGHT

Things you look forward to now . . .

BIBLE VERSE

PROVERBS 15:15 (*NLT*)

. . . for the happy heart, life is a continual feast.

TODAY'S THOUGHT

How did your loved one's death (or other loss) change you?

TODAY: ______

FEELINGS CHECK
Today I feel:

ONE THING I'M GRATEFUL FOR TODAY:

BIBLE VERSE

HOSEA 11:8 (*NIV*)

. . . My heart is changed within me; all my compassion is aroused.

REFLECTIONS

No one can go through deep, significant experiences in life and emerge unchanged. I now view life through a noticeably transformed lens. Different filters have changed my decision-making perspective because of new insights I cannot ignore. New priorities have come into play. My world has changed, and I can't go back. How has your thinking changed?

TODAY: ______

FEELINGS CHECK
Today I feel:

ONE THING I'M GRATEFUL FOR TODAY:

TODAY'S THOUGHT

Describe a lifetime of precious memories you want to hold onto.

BIBLE VERSE

EPHESIANS 5:2 (*NLT*)

Live a life filled with love for others . . .

REFLECTIONS

My special memories include: the birth of our beautiful daughter; struggling to make ends meet while my husband attended college on a football scholarship; moving frequently and building great friendships as a twenty-plus-year military family; growing as a Christian couple; traveling together; enjoying precious time alone and with friends and family; and the ups and downs of a committed marriage. What do you want to remember?

TODAY'S THOUGHT

My new life mission is . . .

BIBLE VERSE

PHILIPPIANS 3:14 (*MSG*)

So let's keep focused on that goal, those of us who want everything God has for us.

TODAY:

FEELINGS CHECK
Today I feel:

ONE THING I'M GRATEFUL FOR TODAY:

REFLECTIONS

My new life mission is to *make a difference*. I want to write books that help others. I want to educate people to change the way they see grief, so it is not a scary, unwelcome, and disagreeable subject. Everyone will face it eventually, so perception matters. Significance is at the heart of my new life mission. What is yours?

TODAY:

FEELINGS CHECK
Today I feel:

ONE THING I'M GRATEFUL FOR TODAY:

TODAY'S THOUGHT

I have a dream to . . .

BIBLE VERSE

Psalm 37:5–6 (*MSG*)

Open up before God, keep nothing back; he'll do whatever needs to be done: He'll validate your life in the clear light of day and stamp you with approval at high noon.

REFLECTIONS

I have a dream to help hurting people reach healing, find new hope in living, and discover the depths of God's love in the process. I have a dream to develop a program to assist people in remapping their lives after losing their mates. I have a dream to see and experience as much of the beauty and wonder of the world as I possibly can. What are your dreams?

TODAY'S THOUGHT

Who or what fuels your hope?
Are you encouraging its growth?

TODAY: ________

FEELINGS CHECK
Today I feel:

ONE THING I'M GRATEFUL FOR TODAY:

BIBLE VERSE

PSALM 139:2–5 (*MSG*)

I'm an open book to you; even from a distance, you know what I'm thinking. You know when I leave and when I get back; I'm never out of your sight. You know everything I'm going to say before I start the first sentence. I look behind me and you're there, then up ahead and you're there, too—your reassuring presence, coming and going.

REFLECTIONS

God fuels my hope. Circumstances change, people (including ourselves) are imperfect, and nothing in the physical world is permanent. Only God is unchangeable, ever present, and always reliable. His promises and love never fail. My hopes are pinned on God. What is your source of hope? Is that connection *growing*?

TODAY:

FEELINGS CHECK
Today I feel:

ONE THING I'M GRATEFUL FOR TODAY:

TODAY'S THOUGHT

Life will *fight* to be heard above your pain. Listen for its voice. Do you hear its whisper?

BIBLE VERSE

PSALM 71:20–21 (*NLT*)

You have allowed me to suffer much hardship, but you will restore me to life again and lift me up from the depths of the earth. You will restore me to even greater honor and comfort me once again.

REFLECTIONS

Can you explain the will to live? This powerful, mysterious force *drives* people to survive despite insurmountable odds. Everyone is born with this power, a voice deep within that whispers to us. Life fights to be heard. Listen. Set your mind and do not let anything stop you. I think the will to live is God's voice nudging, coaxing, encouraging, and strengthening us. *Listen* . . . and respond.

TODAY'S THOUGHT

Do you know someone who needs hope today? Will *you* bring hope to them during their pain?

TODAY:

FEELINGS CHECK
Today I feel:

ONE THING I'M GRATEFUL FOR TODAY:

BIBLE VERSE

ROMANS 15:13 (*NIV*)

May the God of hope fill you with all joy and peace as you trust in him, so that you may overflow with hope by the power of the Holy Spirit.

REFLECTIONS

Do you know someone who needs hope and encouragement to get through a painful time? Will you offer them hope as others did to you? As human beings, we are all connected. We need each other. God wired us that way. Complete the circle of God's love by *being* the person someone else *needs* today.

TODAY:

FEELINGS CHECK
Today I feel:

ONE THING I'M GRATEFUL FOR TODAY:

REFLECTIONS

When you feel depressed or your situation is getting the best of you, look around and find someone to help. A surefire antidote to self-pity is to remove your attention from yourself and direct it toward helping another person. The same is true when you stop thinking about yourself and look to God and His power. He is faithful, always present, and He can do what you cannot.

TODAY'S THOUGHT

It is one of the most beautiful compensations of life, that no man can sincerely try to help another without helping himself.
—Ralph Waldo Emerson

BIBLE VERSE

Psalm 139:7 (*NLT*)

I can never escape from your spirit! I can never get away from your presence!

TODAY'S THOUGHT

It is only possible to live happily ever after on a day-to-day basis.
—Margaret Bonnano

TODAY: ______

FEELINGS CHECK
Today I feel:

ONE THING I'M GRATEFUL FOR TODAY:

BIBLE VERSE

Isaiah 26:3–4 (*NLT*)

You will keep in perfect peace all who trust in you, whose thoughts are fixed on you! Trust in the Lord always, for the Lord God is the eternal Rock.

REFLECTIONS

Don't bite off too much, or look too far into the future. I got myself into trouble when I thought I had to figure out *everything* at once. Focus on whatever is at hand and *live today*. Tomorrow will be here soon enough.

TODAY:

FEELINGS CHECK
Today I feel:

ONE THING I'M GRATEFUL FOR TODAY:

TODAY'S THOUGHT

Don't spend time beating on a wall,
hoping to transform it into a door.
—Dr. Laura Schlessinger

BIBLE VERSE

Hebrews 10:36 (*NLT*)

Patient endurance is what you need now, so you will continue to do God's will. Then you will receive all that he has promised.

REFLECTIONS

Acceptance is key to healing. Anger and denial are common responses to loss, but until you can accept what has happened, you will not get well. Of course, change the things you can. But accepting your unchangeable reality is equally important—in due time.

TODAY'S THOUGHT

You [are] the only person alive who has sole custody of your life . . . . Your entire life . . . . Not just the life of your mind, but the life of your heart. Not just your bank account, but your soul.

—Anna Quindlen

BIBLE VERSE

Matthew 25:29 (*NLT*)

"To those who use well what they are given, even more will be given, and they will have an abundance". . .

TODAY: ______

FEELINGS CHECK
Today I feel:

ONE THING I'M GRATEFUL FOR TODAY:

REFLECTIONS

You, and only you, are in charge of your life. Things beyond your control happen, but you decide how to respond. Believing, loving, thinking, feeling, forgiving, responding, and doing are choices you make. These decisions *build* your life. Choose thoughtfully.

TODAY: ________

FEELINGS CHECK
Today I feel:

ONE THING I'M GRATEFUL FOR TODAY:

TODAY'S THOUGHT

Your best friend and worst enemy are both in this room right now. It's not your neighbor right or left—and it's not God or the devil—it's you.

—Edwin Louis Cole

BIBLE VERSE

Psalm 18:19 (*MSG*)

God made my life complete when I placed all the pieces before him.

REFLECTIONS

You are responsible for your life, but you don't have to do it alone. Be your own best friend and let God do what He does best. Let Him be your loving Father.

TODAY'S THOUGHT

When obstacles arise, you change your direction to reach your goal; you do not change your decision to get there.
—Zig Ziglar

TODAY:

FEELINGS CHECK
Today I feel:

ONE THING I'M GRATEFUL FOR TODAY:

BIBLE VERSE

Galatians 6:9 (*AMP*)

And let us not lose heart and grow weary and faint in acting nobly and doing right, for in due time and at the appointed season we shall reap, if we do not loosen and relax our courage and faint.

REFLECTIONS

You may change directions many times and go forward and backward repeatedly, but remember your ultimate goal. Healing is your objective, and while you make adjustments along the way, your goal never changes.

TODAY: ________

FEELINGS CHECK
Today I feel:

ONE THING I'M GRATEFUL FOR TODAY:

REFLECTIONS

Keep on praying. Prayer *does* make a difference, and your last prayer could be the one that tips the scales. We do not understand what has to happen behind the scenes before God answers our prayers—but He does. As long as we pray, the pipeline stays open and our prayers get more specific. Prayer changes us, too.

TODAY'S THOUGHT

Pray until something happens. God is not ignoring you. He hears every single prayer, but sometimes it's about timing. Your last prayer could be the tipping point.

BIBLE VERSE

Psalm 9:12 (*NLT*)

. . . He does not ignore those who cry to him for help.

TODAY'S THOUGHT

Keep your heart open to dreams. For as long as there's a dream, there is hope, and as long as there is hope, there is joy in living.

—ANONYMOUS

BIBLE VERSE

PROVERBS 23:18 (*NLT*)

For surely you have a future ahead of you; your hope will not be disappointed.

TODAY: ________

FEELINGS CHECK
Today I feel:

____

____

ONE THING I'M GRATEFUL FOR TODAY:

____

____

____

REFLECTIONS

Don't give up. You have a joyful future in God, and He will not let you down. He has everything you need.

TODAY: ________

FEELINGS CHECK
Today I feel:

ONE THING I'M GRATEFUL FOR TODAY:

TODAY'S THOUGHT

BIBLE VERSE

REFLECTIONS

TODAY'S THOUGHT

BIBLE VERSE

TODAY: ______

FEELINGS CHECK
Today I feel:

ONE THING I'M GRATEFUL FOR TODAY:

REFLECTIONS

TODAY:

FEELINGS CHECK
Today I feel:

ONE THING I'M GRATEFUL FOR TODAY:

TODAY'S THOUGHT

BIBLE VERSE

REFLECTIONS

TODAY'S THOUGHT

BIBLE VERSE

TODAY: ______

FEELINGS CHECK
Today I feel:

ONE THING I'M GRATEFUL FOR TODAY:

REFLECTIONS

TODAY:

FEELINGS CHECK
Today I feel:

ONE THING I'M GRATEFUL FOR TODAY:

TODAY'S THOUGHT

BIBLE VERSE

REFLECTIONS

TODAY'S THOUGHT

BIBLE VERSE

TODAY: ________

FEELINGS CHECK
Today I feel:

ONE THING I'M GRATEFUL FOR TODAY:

REFLECTIONS

TODAY: ______

FEELINGS CHECK
Today I feel:

ONE THING
I'M GRATEFUL
FOR TODAY:

TODAY'S THOUGHT

BIBLE VERSE

REFLECTIONS

TODAY'S THOUGHT

BIBLE VERSE

TODAY: ______

FEELINGS CHECK
Today I feel:

ONE THING I'M GRATEFUL FOR TODAY:

REFLECTIONS

TODAY:

FEELINGS CHECK
Today I feel:

ONE THING
I'M GRATEFUL
FOR TODAY:

TODAY'S THOUGHT

BIBLE VERSE

REFLECTIONS

TODAY'S THOUGHT

TODAY:

FEELINGS CHECK
Today I feel:

ONE THING I'M GRATEFUL FOR TODAY:

BIBLE VERSE

REFLECTIONS

TODAY:

FEELINGS CHECK
Today I feel:

ONE THING I'M GRATEFUL FOR TODAY:

TODAY'S THOUGHT

BIBLE VERSE

REFLECTIONS

TODAY'S THOUGHT

BIBLE VERSE

TODAY: ______

FEELINGS CHECK
Today I feel:

ONE THING I'M GRATEFUL FOR TODAY:

REFLECTIONS

TODAY:

FEELINGS CHECK
Today I feel:

ONE THING I'M GRATEFUL FOR TODAY:

TODAY'S THOUGHT

BIBLE VERSE

REFLECTIONS

TODAY'S THOUGHT

BIBLE VERSE

TODAY: ________

FEELINGS CHECK
Today I feel:

ONE THING I'M GRATEFUL FOR TODAY:

REFLECTIONS

TODAY: ______

FEELINGS CHECK
Today I feel:

ONE THING I'M GRATEFUL FOR TODAY:

TODAY'S THOUGHT

BIBLE VERSE

REFLECTIONS

TODAY'S THOUGHT

BIBLE VERSE

TODAY: ______

FEELINGS CHECK
Today I feel:

ONE THING I'M GRATEFUL FOR TODAY:

REFLECTIONS

AFTERWORD

Courage does not always roar. Sometimes courage is the quiet voice at the end of the day saying, "I will try again tomorrow."

—Mary Anne Radmacher

I hope this journal has helped you work through the pain of grief and move closer to accepting and releasing your loss. You have taken a major step toward healing by setting aside time to write about your thoughts and feelings.

If you have not read the book, *STUNNED by Grief: Remapping Your Life When Loss Changes Everything,* I urge you to read it. The book will help you better understand what is happening to you, what to expect, and what to do. It will guide you through the process and support you in your journey. You will read about others' experiences and identify with words of those who have already been where you are now. They made it through. So will you.

I pray that God will give you peace—and fresh hope for the future. Thank you for allowing me to go along on your journey.

I wish you God's best.

Judy Brizendine

He [God] has made everything beautiful in its time.
He has also planted eternity in men's hearts and minds [a divinely implanted sense of a purpose working through the ages which nothing under the sun but God alone can satisfy] . . .

—Ecclesiastes 3:11 (*AMP*)

APPENDIX

FEELINGS CHECKLIST

Abandoned
Able
Abused
Accepted
Adaptable
Adored
Agitated
Agreeable
Alienated
Alive
Angry
Anxious
Apologetic
Ashamed
Assured
Authentic
Bitter
Blessed
Bored
Brave
Brokenhearted
Busy
Calm
Capable
Cautious
Centered
Chaotic
Cheerful
Cherished
Compassionate
Complacent
Confused
Connected
Content
Courageous
Creative
Daring
Defeated
Defensive
Delighted
Depressed
Dissatisfied
Distracted
Distraught
Disturbed
Doubtful
Eager
Empathetic
Empowered
Empty
Energetic
Enthusiastic
Envious
Excited
Exhausted
Faithful
Fearful
Forgiven
Forgotten
Fragmented
Friendly
Frustrated
Fulfilled
Generous

Good	Lost	Refreshed	Stressed
Grateful	Loved	Regretful	Tense
Grounded	Loving	Relaxed	Terrified
Guilty	Lucky	Resentful	Thankful
Happy	Misunderstood	Rested	Tired
Homesick	Nervous	Restless	Treasured
Hopeful	Obedient	Sad	Trusting
Hostile	Offended	Safe	Uncomfortable
Humble	Open	Satisfied	Understood
Hurt	Optimistic	Scared	Unfocused
Hypocritical	Outraged	Scattered	Unhappy
Ignored	Overwhelmed	Secure	Unsettled
Impatient	Patient	Self-centered	Uplifted
Inferior	Peaceful	Self-confident	Valued
Insecure	Powerful	Selfish	Victorious
Inspired	Prideful	Sensitive	Vulnerable
Interested	Protected	Serene	Weak
Irritated	Puzzled	Shunned	Weary
Isolated	Quiet	Snug	Weepy
Jealous	Reassured	Somber	Wonderful
Joyful	Rebellious	Spirited	Worried
Lethargic	Reconciled	Stable	Wounded

ENDNOTES

Judy Brizendine, *STUNNED by Grief: Remapping Your Life When Loss Changes Everything* (Lake Forest, CA: BennettKnepp Publishing, 2011).

Article by Kevin Kelly, Editor of the *Whole Earth Review* (based on a telephone interview with Norman Cousins). *Whole Earth Review,* No. 61, Winter 1988.

SOURCES ON LAUGHTER, HUMOR THERAPY, AND HEALTH

Godfrey, Jodi R., M.S., R.D. "Toward Optimal Health: The Experts Discuss Therapeutic Humor," *Journal of Women's Health* 13, no. 5 (2004): 474–79.

ONLINE ARTICLES/RESOURCES/REFERENCES:

Bennett, Sandy. (November 1, 2001). Irvine researcher studying the connection between laughter and health. *OC Metro Business.* http://www. ocmetro.com/archives/ocmetro_2001/metro 110101/hot25/berk.html. [Note: online archives currently go back only to 2002]

Diggs, Tammie S. Laughter: Is It Healthy? http://hiwaay.net/~garson/laughter.htm.

Fusco, S. CEC Article—Laughter, Jest for the Health of It. http://www.aquacert.org/cec42005.pdf.

Gallozzi, Chuck. Benefits of Laughter. http://www.personal-development.com/chuck/laughter.htm.

How moods affect our health. (December 11, 2007). *The Independent.* http://www.independent.co.uk/life-style/health-and-wellbeing/healthy-living/how-moods-affect-our-health-764289.html.

Humor Therapy. http://www.holistic-online.com/stress/stress_humor.htm.

Kay, Dr., and Max, Dr. (October 28, 2007). Integrative Way: Go ahead and laugh—it's good for you. *The Sacramento Bee.* http://www.sacbee.com/107/story/454398.html.

Koerner, Pete. The Secret to Happiness. *Ezine Articles.* http://ezinearticles.com/?The-Secret-to-Happiness&id=1055830.

Laughter: The Ageless Prescription for Good Health. http://justlaughter.com/ageless_prescription.htm.

Laughter research conducted at LLUMC. (March 11, 1999). *Loma Linda University School of Medicine News.* http://www.llu.edu/pages/news/today/mar99/sm.htm.

Lindeman, Leslie, Kemp, Gina, M.A., and Segal, Jeanne, Ph.D. (September 26, 2007). Humor, Laughter and Health: Bringing More Humor and Laughter into Our Lives. http://www.helpguide.org/life/humor_laughter_health.htm.

Love, Joe. Developing Your Sense of Humor. *Ezine Articles.* http://ezinearticles.com/?Developing-Your-Sense-Of-Humor&id=181073.

Reynolds, Joyce K. The Many Benefits of Laughter. *CoachTALK.* Volume III, May 2002. http://www.jkr.net/newsletter/coachtalk2002-05.htm

Scott, Elizabeth, M.S. The Stress Management and Health Benefits of Laughter. (October 7, 2009). About.com: Stress Management. http://stress.about.com/od/stresshealth/a/laughter.htm.

Therapeutic Benefits of Laughter. Holistic online. http://www.holisticon-line.com/Humor_Therapy/humor_therapy_benefits.htm.

Why a good laugh inspires a better life. *The Standard* (December 20, 2007). http://216.180.252.4/archives/index.php?mnu=details&id=1143979151&catid=318.

HOW TO CONTACT THE AUTHOR

To reach Judy Brizendine and find additional resources,
please visit the website:
www.stunnedbygrief.com

Or write to:
Judy Brizendine
c/o BennettKnepp Publishing
P.O. Box 296
Lake Forest, CA 92609-0296

If you would like to tell me about your experience or
give feedback on the book or journal,
I'd love to hear from you.
My email address is:
jbriz@stunnedbygrief.com

Additional copies of *STUNNED by Grief* and
the *STUNNED by Grief Journal*
can be ordered online:
www.stunnedbygrief.com

BennettKnepp
PUBLISHING

Lake Forest, CA

BennettKnepp Publishing is dedicated to producing books that effect positive change in the lives of individuals and the world. Our goal is to engage, inform, delight, and transform people through the written word.

We value our readers' opinions and encourage your feedback. To offer suggestions or make comments about our books, please write to us.

BennettKnepp Publishing
P.O. Box 296
Lake Forest, CA 92609-0296

www.bennettknepp.com

This book is available at special quantity discounts for bulk purchases by businesses, organizations, churches, and special-interest groups. Customized books, booklets, or excerpts can be created to fit specific needs. For information, please contact the publisher.

ABOUT THE AUTHOR

Judy Brizendine is a business professional whose life radically changed course after the tragic, sudden death of her husband. That experience, along with facilitating grief-support workshops, helped her define a new, practical, and personal approach to grief.